C000171365

"Technology has expanded the space o
Complexity has become a feature of ou
working and living in a state of 'cog
alone is not enough to solve the problem
new world. In this beautiful book, Kari.. ....
feminine leadership, the only approach capable of successfully facing the
diversity of the current world. An absolute must read."

> – **Prof. Dr. Roberto Panzarani**, University LUMSA,
> Rome, Italy; CEO of Panzarani Innovation and
> Associates; author of *Innovare il pensiero:
> i modelli di business in un'economia volatile*

"As a female leader in diverse settings, I am always searching for ways to
connect vision, people and action. Karin Jironet invites us to examine our
role as leaders through Dante's journey in Purgatory: a perfect metaphor
for freeing ourselves to honour virtue and help us to be the leaders that
we want to be."

> – **Deepa Patel**, international advisor on refugee issues and chair
> of multiple charities, London, United Kingdom

"Karin Jironet is a leader of leaders. In this new edition of her
groundbreaking work, *Feminine Leadership*, she offers a clearsighted
and up-to-date perspective on present problems globe-wide and a
correspondingly large horizon of future possibilities. We must all –
however gendered – become leaders. This is a book for everyone."

> **Murray Stein, Ph.D.**, author of *Jung's Map of the Soul*,
> Zurich, Switzerland

Feminine Leadership

This revised and updated edition of *Feminine Leadership: Personal Development Beyond Polarities* illustrates how contemporary leaders may seek to renew the very notion of leadership through their own personal development.

In an accessible and engaging style, Karin Jironet demonstrates the process of personal transformation using Dante's seven sins and virtues, explains the value of psychology and spirituality for leadership roles, and presents a pioneering and refreshed vision of leadership that meets present global demands for social cohesion and sustainability. This revised edition contains updates throughout and presents personal narratives that illustrate the seven virtues of leadership practice in our current socio-political context. This book addresses questions on how leadership is defined, exercised and communicated in contemporary society.

Feminine Leadership will be of great interest to all leaders and professionals who wish to familiarize themselves with personal leadership development and learn how Jungian theory has been put into practice in this field.

Karin Jironet is a theologian and Jungian psychoanalyst working with executive leadership development. For more than twenty years, she has offered immersion retreats in the Netherlands, Italy, India and Switzerland.

Feminine Leadership

Personal Development Beyond Polarities

Second Edition

Karin Jironet

Routledge
Taylor & Francis Group

LONDON AND NEW YORK

Second edition published 2020
by Routledge
2 Park Square, Milton Park, Abingdon, Oxon, OX14 4RN

and by Routledge
52 Vanderbilt Avenue, New York, NY 10017

Routledge is an imprint of the Taylor & Francis Group, an informa business

© 2020 Karin Jironet

The right of Karin Jironet to be identified as author of this work has been asserted by her in accordance with sections 77 and 78 of the Copyright, Designs and Patents Act 1988.

All rights reserved. No part of this book may be reprinted or reproduced or utilised in any form or by any electronic, mechanical, or other means, now known or hereafter invented, including photocopying and recording, or in any information storage or retrieval system, without permission in writing from the publishers.

Trademark notice: Product or corporate names may be trademarks or registered trademarks, and are used only for identification and explanation without intent to infringe.

First edition published by Routledge 2011

British Library Cataloguing-in-Publication Data
A catalogue record for this book is available from the British Library

Library of Congress Cataloging-in-Publication Data
Names: Jironet, Karin, author.
Title: Feminine leadership : personal development
    beyond polarities / Karin Jironet.
Description: Second edition. | Milton Park, Abingdon,
    Oxon ; New York, NY : Routledge, 2020. | Includes
    bibliographical references and index.
Identifiers: LCCN 2019043337 | ISBN 9781138598225
    (hardback) | ISBN 9781138598263 (paperback) |
    ISBN 9780429486487 (ebook)
Subjects: LCSH: Leadership in women. |
    Jungian psychology.
Classification: LCC BF637.L4 J57 2020 |
    DDC 158/.4—dc23
LC record available at https://lccn.loc.gov/2019043337

ISBN: 978-1-138-59822-5 (hbk)
ISBN: 978-1-138-59826-3 (pbk)
ISBN: 978-0-429-48648-7 (ebk)

Typeset in Times New Roman
by Apex CoVantage, LLC

This book is dedicated to Elena and Esmée

Contents

Acknowledgements

Many people have contributed to this book's journey to maturation – and to mine. There are too many to name and thank here, but I do want to mention a few individuals in particular. Cultural and societal factors, too, have played a key role in the evolution of this book. The places I live, for example, and the opportunities I've been granted as a result. I note my heartfelt thanks for the numerous factors, seen and unseen, which have guided my life and my choices, and shaped my views.

Among the individuals to whom I offer my gratitude are my clients and my colleagues. These professionals – lawyers, medical specialists, other healthcare professionals, entrepreneurs, investors, politicians, education specialists and finance professionals – have shown commitment to continuous self-encountering and service of communities, which has formed an inspiration and a beacon of light for over 20 years of practice. My special thanks and respect goes to the interviewees who brought such sensitive and unique stories, which I sincerely hope will prove inspiring to many leaders on the path of practicing modern, feminine leadership. Thanks also to Bercan Günel for sharing insights and perspectives flowing forth from her wealth of experience.

The psychological and philosophical theory and knowledge fundamental to the book has been taught and transmitted by eminent scholars and practitioners in multiple fields. I think firstly of my lifetime Sufi guide Karimbakhsh Witteveen, along with Sufi and other friends who practice spirituality with an endless commitment to truth. And of my teachers, analysts and supervisors in analytical psychology, I especially thank Zurich-based Bernard Sartorius, Connie Steiner and Murray Stein, who with angelic patience commented on early drafts.

There would not be a book without its readers. And there would not have been any book at all without my editor Susannah Frearson at Routledge, who offered a warm breeze of confidence with her every response to my emails and revisions, even when deadlines had become past tense. Many thanks also to Heather Evans at Routledge, for all support and encouragement.

My heartfelt, profound and sincere thank you to Sally Clarke who with amazing competence and stamina – from all corners of the world – has helped with research, feedback and text suggestions that have been indispensable for the formation of the book.

I thank my two children Disa and Filip, two stepchildren Maaike and Anouk, and their partners, as well as my two granddaughters Elena and Esmée for granting me so much real joy and wonder. And for their openness to comfort, conversation, understanding, forgiveness, play, love and learning from "us", the way we are together, all the while balancing instinct with intellect.

Thank you Harry Starren for your enduring support and wisdom – I cannot help but smile as I write this.

All interviews have been published with consent of the interviewee.

Chapter 1

Introduction

Why feminine leadership matters to everyone

Since the first edition of this book was published in 2011, discussions around what it means to be a leader have vastly evolved. On a political level, the rise of populism around the globe has seen a significant change in the rhetoric of elected officials. In the corporate sphere, the traditional, male-dominated hierarchical model has eroded, replaced by a flatter, more open and direct dynamic. Discrimination is a long way from being eradicated, but minorities are more vocal – and their voices are having more impact – than ever before. There are more women in powerful *positions* – managers, politicians, councilors, police commissioners, judges and CEOs – in our society today than ever before. However, the stereotypical perception of a powerful *person* remains unchanged: "our mental, cultural template for a powerful person remains resolutely male."[1]

Despite advances over the centuries, Western culture continues to exclude women from an equal conversation (and the feminine from any leadership model) and instead silences them, to the detriment of a swiftly shifting playing field, as well as – deeply ironically – to the societies and organizations in which leaders operate. The structure that has been tightly coded as male for millennia does not allow space for the feminine. In order to facilitate truly equal and balanced leadership forms and frameworks, fundamental transformation in the collective comprehension of power is required. "It means decoupling [power] from public prestige. It means, above all, thinking about power as an attribute or even a verb (to power), not as a possession . . . the ability to be effective, to make a difference in the world, and the right to be taken seriously, together, as much as individually."[2]

In the Netherlands, which formed my professional base for a few decades, the statistics regarding gender equality in management and public-sector leadership remain unimpressive. The number of Dutch women in executive roles is significantly lower on the scale compared to the Scandinavian countries.[3] However, Dutch women in private and public sectors no longer operate within the framework of a stereotypical structure and mentality. And this points to a gradual but continuing shift in perception and awareness of what a powerful person looks like.

Awareness is growing of the interconnectedness between personal development and collective evolution. The individual's personal development impacts the collective consciousness, which stimulates personal development, and so on. Christof Koch, one of today's most well-known experts on consciousness, contends that all living things, including animals, nature and the elements, are able to perceive and feel. He writes in *Consciousness: Here, There and Everywhere* that consciousness is "an intrinsic, fundamental property of reality."[4]

This is a profoundly empowering concept. Although group dynamics will always remain important to human experience, the individual has the capacity to impact the world – by working on themselves, and evolving, the fabric of humanity is changed. Viewed through this lens, there is nothing to fear about the increasing individuation[5] in society – it is a shift from relying on external signals to guide our beliefs and behavior, towards greater awareness, wholeness and use of intuition. Leaders can proactively benefit themselves, their organization and the world at large when they are ready to act with the courage to discard old culturally bound fears, and face "new" fears that might arise, such as being absorbed by an unknown cloud collective, with conscious awareness of the power of interconnectivity and interdependence.

The global developments to which we are currently bearing witness, especially in terms of financial systems and corporate governance, along with transitions in areas ranging from politics to welfare, require that "leadership" acquires a new and different meaning. It is critical that the focus now shifts towards the microcosm of the individual human being, their intrinsic motivating force, and their readiness and ability to connect and create relationships from the core. In a global marketplace, leadership means skillful interaction with others based on a firm grounding of understanding the unity of all. No longer can we simply adjust a position to the particular requirements of a specific organization at any given time; these kinds of knee-jerk, reactive decisions are inherently flawed because factors such as gender, generation and race, and the respective biases around these factors, inevitably interfere with truly wise judgment. Instead, we must have the courage to lift our gaze from the immediate problem to be solved, and instead understand wholeness and interconnectedness. Powerful leadership commences when the internal forms the core starting point for external action, rather than actions being taken one after the other, simply out of habit and despite questionable or abominable consequences. As our past bears out, these actions easily follow one another quite automatically, until a course of action is formed and history has been made. Many an unnecessary tragedy has unfolded, many an unneeded war has raged, primarily as a result of reflex, fear-based decisions that constitute a "re-action" to the external, rather than an understanding of interconnectedness and the powerful wisdom of intuition.

This human tendency, to allow stereotype, superstition and ideological agendas to prevail when a clear understanding of what is going on – an answer to the unanswerable "why"? – is lacking, is nothing new. For example, during both the various credit crises that played out two millennia ago, and the credit and economic crises of our time, the human reaction is one of surprise, shock and panic. The challenge for leaders in this environment is in a sense what it has always been – to see the bigger picture and act in the interests of the organization as a whole rather than out of selfish or individual motives. What's new – and extremely exciting – is that consciousness is increasingly being viewed and accepted as the best possible means of meeting this challenge.[6]

This is not a contradiction in terms – for leaders to move to an internal starting point for behavior and thinking, rather than a reactive posture, but also to see the bigger picture and act in the interests of the organization as a whole. It is not a choice between individual and the group. Because, when one fully understands and experiences the innate interconnectedness of all, and the power of the intuition, one sees that intuition is not of the self, but of that interconnected whole. It is heartening to see how this consciousness-based means of decision-making is increasingly being embraced in the corporate and commercial world.

Feminine leadership is a model for stepping into a new modus operandi. More on why and how later. Let's take a look now at developments that have radically impacted the leadership framework and what constitutes valuable leadership in the social context. Firstly, the movement towards manifest diversity, not only prompted by massive demographic shifts, but perhaps more so by (or at least in conjunction with) a reappraisal of value and power as social indicators. Secondly, a glimpse at technology-driven developments occurring in all major sectors of society – healthcare, education, politics, families, religion – and how

these developments bring into question labor relations and employability, and give rise to new ways of working. And finally, I address what the
human factor means for business today, and tomorrow.

Diversity

In business, politics and society generally, diversity is a buzzword that
verges on hackneyed. Nevertheless, its meaning is broader and more
potent than ever. Change is the only constant, both as individuals and as
a society. For current purposes, diversity is not simply a matter of having more women in powerful roles. Personal and organizational success
today depends on diversity in every aspect: age, background, gender,
religion, experience, stance, race, perspective.[7]

Embracing diversity itself is a feminine concept, as it draws on our
capacity to be inclusive, open and non-aggressive. It demands that we
act without fear and let go of judgments and presumptions that can be
held quite subconsciously – hence the importance of inner work referred
to above, and self-reflection which I delve into below.

Gender – a new concept

The male/female dichotomy is a thing of the past. It is now scientifi-
cally evident that our delineation of humanity into two neat categories of
gender is false.[8] This is liberating, no matter how you identify, because it
speaks to a broader awareness that the definitions to which humans have
unquestioningly adhered for centuries are capable of being undone, over-
turned and rewritten.[9] This profound shift in perspective also underscores
that the arbitrary terms "male" and "female" are far from all-or-nothing
polarization. Feminine leadership is not just about woman who lead. It's
about every leader, regardless of gender, utilizing – embracing – the feminine qualities that will make them better leaders and better human beings.

Experience over security

The days of leaving university, commencing a graduate role in that field,
and working until a golden watch upon retirement are gone. Today's
workforce is more mobile, flexible, critical, intelligent, diverse and empow-
ered. While they suffer from lower job security than previous generations, they are also less loyal as employees. If they find themselves
unhappy they won't just suck it up: they will seek the guidance of a life
coach and readily explore other opportunities that better meet their goals.

Simple monetary remuneration is no longer sufficient to attract and retain quality employees – today's employers must offer meaning, engagement and respect if they want to draw the best people. It's as much about life experience as it is about the paycheck.

Higher (and higher) education

Millennials and members of Generation Z are far more likely than their predecessors to start their own businesses, believe in their ideas and pursue a high-level tertiary education. This is partly due to the extremely competitive labor market, and the increase in higher education participation over recent decades. While a basic university qualification would mean access to comfortable public service positions a few decades ago, today a master's degree is the norm.

This increase in competition means higher levels of stress and anxiety among youth, as well as the double-edged sword of increased freedom – the privilege of a greater array of options and possibilities, laced with the pressure to make the "right" decision from the enormous range, and maximize every opportunity presented.

Age is just a number

Today we are witnessing multiple generations (five is not unusual) collaborating in the workforce. And while previously intergenerational learning tended to flow from the older to the younger, today's digital generation have as much to offer their more experienced colleagues as the other way around. The younger generations are anxious and stressed about the issues that confront the world – climate change, gender inequality, wealth distribution – as well as their own career path and fulfilment. They experience the tension between the inner and outer life, exemplified by the young senior executive who works 70 hours per week, goes on an expensive week-long retreat, posts about its healing qualities on Instagram, then returns unquestioningly to the 70-hour working week.

Younger generations experience the angst of reduced job security amid a fast-changing playing field and increased pressure to achieve the nebulous concept that is "success". An increasing number of younger people are rejecting the traditional parameters of success as heralded by their elders, and seeking out non-traditional or even multiple careers. Accountant, and rock-climbing instructor. Office assistant, and yoga teacher, and amateur DJ. Members of older generations who have the confidence to be inspired, rather than intimidated, by this wisdom have much to gain from interaction with, and even adoption of aspects of, the mindset of Generation Z.

The impact of technology

Technology is changing at an exponential rate, and both the technology itself and the rate of change impacts our work and private lives immensely.[10] Every device we buy is outdated before we leave the store; new software is constantly being designed and refined in pursuit of an optimal user experience. This impacts the workplace and its leaders, logistically and culturally.

Trite notions regarding leadership capabilities and their aggressive application have dominated the leadership discourse for such a long time that attention for intuition, and a deeper understanding of the nature of things (focus, attunement, beauty, energy), have been sidelined. It's exciting to see what a powerful and positive role tech can play in subverting this paradigm. Artificial intelligence, fast-paced development in other areas of tech as well as environmental, financial and demographic shifts create a new context, to which leaders can only adapt through an alternative way of thinking and perceiving.

Fear of the impact of AI on our existence is outdated: our lives are already permeated by artificial intelligence, whether we are aware (or approve) of it or not. Our smartphones and tablets are practically a part of us, and our online presence is both curated and refined but also underpinned by masses of data we provide through our online behavior. Indeed, it is questionable whether we should still "describe the Internet as 'virtual' or 'unreal' space any longer".[11] The collection of infinite amounts of data regarding who we are – or at least, how we identify ourselves – is facilitated by the willingness with which we embrace technologies that make our lives seemingly easier and provide a sense of control over our environment. So, while technological developments that enable our thoughts to be immediately transcribed, recorded or instantly transmitted might seem slightly creepy now, any technology which we perceive as expanding our sense of control or making our lives easier will almost certainly be rapidly embraced, irrespective of any Orwellian connotations.

A self-learning chess champion

AlphaZero, a self-learning algorithm that plays chess, "displays a breed of intellect that humans have not seen before".[12] It has insight, it understands the game. Contrary to its predecessor, Stockfish, the reigning computer chess world champion which famously beat Kasparov, AlphaZero hasn't been programmed with a massive amount of expert chess moves – it is truly self-learning. And the properties which enabled AlphaZero to win thousands of chess games over Stockfish, without a single loss, are intuition and selective attention, knowing what to think about and what not to. It plays beautifully and – interestingly – intuitively, "with the finesse of a virtuoso".

Kasparov himself states that AlphaZero "reflects the truth" about the game rather than "the priorities and prejudices of programmers".[13] The public fascination with AlphaZero – it's even considered to be romantic – lies in its human way of acting. Is it easier to admire the computer than to honor our own beauty, intuition and proficiency?

Using technology with consciousness

Adoption of technology is critical to workplace success, and to attracting the brightest minds, who are capable of embracing the possibilities technology offers. Balance is key, and successful use of technology is like the workplace towards which modern society is evolving: it's much more about efficient interaction than hours clocked. However, there is a heightened tension created by the incredible external focus of social media that has contributed to something of a collective identity crisis.[14] If you don't post an event to Twitter or Instagram – did it even happen?

The stated goal of Facebook is to create "meaningful groups" with a view to "bringing us closer together and building a global community".[15] However, making social media a "private" experience[16] is contrary to the principles of individuation which are critical to our evolution as a society. Something about the current means of interface will need to change substantially for these to evolve from online cliques hurling abuse at one other, or – just as dangerously – only interacting with like-minded people, and thereby eliminating diversity from their lives. The end goal might be "the eradication of all boundaries separating one mind from another",[17] but social media in its current manifestation, is clearly not going to achieve this. However, when we consider the exponential rate at which technology is developing, it is fascinating to contemplate what social media will mean, and how it will serve and define us, in a decade from now.

In terms of social media usage, a disciplined approach is certainly required. Strong leaders intrinsically know when they need to speak to someone in real life and when a WhatsApp call will suffice. Aware of its well-documented pitfalls, leaders will also strictly limit their use of social media. It's not something to fill time when bored, or to interact with during a conversation or while working out: there has to be some underlying, positive purpose. For most leaders, a healthy, balanced approach works best, without succumbing to either total disconnection[18] or addiction.[19]

The evolving labor market

Dutch leaders and families show a forward-thinking approach in the labor market which is currently being explored in other countries. For example, part-time work, which facilitates focus on career, and family, and civic or social roles, has been a cornerstone of the Dutch labor market for decades. Flexibility in the workplace, and in how we allocate time and attend to our responsibilities as leaders and as humans, is key. It enables leaders to form an important part of the labor market requiring less compromise to other aspects of their lives than in countries where it's full-time or nothing.

Particularly among Generation Z, working part-time is not viewed as an inhibition to career growth and personal development, but as a powerful tool to ensure that they can have well-rounded, multifaceted and truly fulfilling lives. This younger generation doesn't want to "have it all", in the traditional sense. Their priorities are authenticity, personal growth and a sense of purpose. Stability and security are no longer the primary driving forces: Generation Z wants to contribute to society by tackling the causes of problems, seeking social solutions while living according to personally held values, and – pointedly – not those dictated by society.[20]

But how do you find out about your core, your professional calling, your hidden gifts and those less attractive aspects of your personality? How do you ensure your purpose manifest in vocations and relationships?

Self-reflection

Self-reflection is the capacity to look within at our own machinations, motivations and biases to identify, and where appropriate adapt, the way we think and judge, how we make decisions and the behavior that we exhibit as a result. It emphasizes inner processes rather than external results. Unfortunately, in contrast, much management literature today is driven by a focus on the individual's capacity to manoeuvre according to external expectations and predetermined objectives: the company's stipulated financial or HR goals, for example, or pressure from superiors to adopt a particular position. This leads to focus on the service of external goals, which quickly becomes an embedded and unquestioned norm. Self-reflection is essential for leadership success. This is because transformations experienced around the globe – including those that are caused by a shift in human consciousness – require of leaders the power to surrender structures of the past rather than clinging to them.

Self-realization, which may follow on from self-reflection, is more than a technique, and human consciousness and sensitivity remain – so far – exclusive to humanity. It is a real thing, not an abstract notion, because it is informed by individuality and embedded in experience. To lead with that consciousness and sensitivity any individual must acknowledge the gift of being human as a fundamental resource, which, when put into service and fully utilized will create meaningful relationships in which self-reflection in proximity can be practiced at work.

The central focus in this book is on the individual leader's experiences and how these can be used to reveal new, effective and positive ways of leading. It introduces a perspective that integrates the feminine into corporate leadership in the form of relational competences, meta-rational faculties for decision-making, proximity with and tolerance for the multifaceted personalities that make up the organization. Leaders today have the opportunity to harness a new model of leadership, one that is founded on an ongoing awareness of the workings of the inner life, its external manifestations and how it matters for interpersonal relationships in the workplace.

An inside view on feminine leadership

This book examines what we have come to know as "personal development" from the perspective of *Purgatory*, part two of Dante's *The Divine Comedy*. Dante's work represents an archetypal image of a life journey towards freedom from false images of the self. Apart from its many other brilliant qualities, this journey of imagination shows us how fundamental and deeply rooted our strictly personal reflections actually are. Even today there is recognition of a universality that we take part in and yet experience individually.

For the purpose of this book, Dante's *Purgatory* must be conceived of as a pointer to the world of major feelings, shared by all people and expressed in this form in the Western Christian tradition. It points to the paramount dilemmas of an existence in duality. No matter how much we hope to understand what Dante transmits, there are benefits simply from engaging with him, from feeling his sincere struggle and honest resistance and amazement at all he encounters and experiences. Once this journey of personal exploration and development begins, it becomes a process of utter bewilderment.

Dante's journey through *Purgatory* and his confrontation with the seven sins and their corresponding virtues, two sides of the same coin, is a powerful metaphor for your personal journey. I show how these metaphors are profoundly instructive in how best to lead, to understand the potent dynamics of the transformational processes that occur intrinsic to leadership roles, and to recognize the same at play in others.

What lies behind each pair of opposites is a fundamental energy or quality of relating. It is the way you move into contact with another person or an object, something outside of yourself. However, whatever attitude you hold, it is ultimately governed by your relationship with yourself. This relationship with yourself, in turn, is formed by your personality and how you were treated and related to as a child and later in life. Without self-reflection you are led to believe that you are as people have seen you, addressed you, judged you. That your worth is determined by this. But you are more than that.

Exploration of these metaphors for your personal journey will clarify and strengthen your leadership abilities, and will foster increased creativity and candid interpersonal communication in leaders' workplaces.

While this book focuses primarily on leaders in the context of Western society, I want to emphasize that the aspects of feminine leadership explored in the chapters to come are applicable in infinite situations, and to us all. As the subtitle suggests, this journey through Purgatory on which we find ourselves is indeed a global one; it touches all individuals, not just leaders at corporate entities in Europe, for example. The framework for personal development and its application through leadership I use here is generally organizational settings familiar to those living in Western society. However, the means of taking this global journey, and seeing it through to its destination, is not limited to this framework. There are arguably as many ways to self-realization as there are human beings, and personal development can be achieved by numerous approaches. Feminine leadership has universal application for all those seeking to self-know, self-realize and lead.

A great deal has occurred in the eight years since this book was first published. This edition of the book has been carefully updated for today's world. It also includes exclusive interviews with leaders setting out what feminine leadership means for them, personally and professionally.

Their wisdom, and insight into an array of important topics, many of which I have touched on in this introduction, offers practical, relatable and heartfelt experience and guidance for adopting feminine leadership as individuals and, in turn, as a society.

During the course of conducting these interviews, intended to form a kind of case study to bring each virtue and hence each chapter to life, I found myself deeply inspired by the articulate, profound and very real and relevant perspectives of these seven senior executives. Each of them shared such a bounty of important points that touched on all seven of the virtues. Nevertheless, each seemed to speak particularly to one of the virtues, and was allocated accordingly. I hope you find their wisdom (and wit), as well as Dante's example of self-reflection and realization, inspiring for your own journey in feminine leadership.

Notes

1 Beard (2018), p. 53.
2 Beard (2018), p. 87.
3 https://apolitical.co/solution_article/ranked-mapped-women-public-sector-leadership-around-world/www3.weforum.org/docs/WEF_GGGR_2018.pdf
4 Tononi, G. and Koch, C. (2015). Consciousness: Here, there and everywhere? *Philosophical Transactions of the Royal Society B: Biological Sciences*, 370: 20140167. http://dx.doi.org/10.1098/rstb.2014.0167
5 Individuation is term coined by C.G. Jung to signify the journey of psycho-spiritual development that leads to self-realization. When the true self is realized, it becomes the platform for a person's interaction with the world, and is therefore inherently interwoven with all else in creation.
6 see e.g., Davies (2019), Cooper Ramo (2016), Laloux (2014).
7 www.forbes.com/sites/rsmdiscovery/2018/08/22/why-workplace-diversity-is-so-important-and-why-its-so-hard-to-achieve/#21db2f5b3096
8 See www.nytimes.com/interactive/2019/06/28/us/pride-identity.html?te=1&nl=top-stories&emc=edit_ts_20190628?campaign_id=61&instance_id=10567&segment_id=14769&user_id=33e13224063954a08c3c270cb77e bb9f&regi_id=7149614120190628
9 www.nytimes.com/interactive/2019/06/28/us/pride-identity.html?em_pos=large&ref=headline&te=1&nl=top-stories&emc=edit_ts_20190628?campaign_id=61&instance_id=10567&segment_id=14769&user_id=33e13 224063954a08c3c270cb77ebb9f&regi_id=71496141edit_ts_20190628
10 Kromme, C. (2017).
11 Davies (2019), p. 188.
12 www.nytimes.com/2018/12/26/science/chess-artificial-intelligence.html
13 https://science.sciencemag.org/content/362/6419/1087.full
14 Fukuyama, F. (2018). *Identity: Contemporary Identity Politics and the Struggle for Recognition*. London: Profile Books.
15 Davies, W. (2019). *Nervous States: Democracy and the Decline of Reason*. London: W. W. Norton & Company, p. 177.

16 www.bbc.com/news/technology-48835250
17 Davies, W. (2019). *Nervous States: Democracy and the Decline of Reason.* London: W. W. Norton & Company.
18 www.refinery29.com/en-gb/2017/09/173223/zadie-smith-social-media-writing
19 www.gurlstalk.com/gurls/article/my-instagram-addiction/
20 Seemiller, C. and Grace, M. (2018). *Generation Z: A Century in the Making.* Oxon: Routledge.

Chapter 2

The Divine Comedy

Dante's life was characterized by a personal struggle for truth and spiritual growth through integration and continuous renewal. It is worthwhile looking not only at his work but also at Dante's biography because it throws light on the soul's journey as described in *Purgatory*. So, on the one hand, it is an imaginary journey, while on the other hand, looking at Dante's life, it is also real. In addition, within Dante's biography we find a story of overcoming obstacles not by fighting or proactively attacking, which would be more of a masculine discourse, but rather by yielding, reflecting and relating, a more feminine approach. Dante overcame his feelings of being an outsider by exploring the hidden core beneath the surfaces of obvious opposites; he made the effort to open himself to them and was thus united within himself. That is different from cleaning and sweeping away external obstacles.

In *Purgatory* all sins and virtues are explained in terms of their relationship to love, the way of the heart. This appeals to leaders practicing feminine leadership, which is mainly geared towards relationships. Let us look at some aspects of Dante's biography that reveal how he arrived at this. Dante Alighieri was born in Florence in May or June 1265 and died in Ravenna in 1321. He was one of the most influential thinkers and philosophers of his age and one of the greatest poets of all times. Dante went from rationality and idealism towards freedom from form, and an experience of bliss and grace through love. Dante was a true mystic, and as such he defined steps to personal self-realization that we can find in many different cultures and traditions, steps that seem to carry a universal truth. His work was in many ways an example of his life, and *The Divine Comedy* an autobiography.

Life and leadership

Dante was born and brought up in Florence as a Roman Catholic. His mother died when he was aged between six and nine. His father soon remarried and fathered two more children: a boy and a girl. Dante's father died when Dante was about 18.

In May 1274, when he was nine, he met Beatrice Portinari, who was then eight. The encounter left an everlasting impression on him. Although they never really developed the contact, and later on both were married to other people, it was his feelings for Beatrice that Dante turned to for exaltation and sublime inspiration. Even after her death in 1290, Beatrice remained the source of inspiration for Dante. She, together with Dante's guide Virgil, are the central characters in the *Comedy* and his point of orientation in other major works.

In Dante's time Italy was not a united country, but a collection of mostly small city states. Power struggles among noble families were a constant source of wars between states and of turmoil and civil war within them.

There were tensions between two great religious and political factions, the Guelfs and the Ghibellines, which competed for control over Florence. In essence, they represented two opposing positions with regard to the power of the pope. The Guelfs fought for the papacy and political autonomy, whereas the Ghibellines supported centralization and the Holy Roman Emperor. Like his father, Dante was affiliated with the Guelfs and he served as a soldier and fought at Campaldino in 1289. He held several political offices, among them ambassador to San Giminiano in 1299.

In 1285 Dante married Gemma Donati, a member of a prominent Florentine Guelf family active in Florentine cultural and civic life. Around this time the Guelfs lost power in Florence, and gradually internal power struggles and differences in allegiance to the papacy split the group.

In 1301, at the instigation of Pope Boniface VIII, the faction within the Guelfs to which Dante adhered, the Whites, was overruled. Together with a few other leading Guelfs, Dante was exiled from Florence in 1302. He briefly joined the Ghibellines, and then commenced a 20-year journey, living in various places, mainly in Tuscany and northern parts of Italy, until his death. During this period Dante became convinced that the worst sinners are the ones who are indifferent in times of moral decline and crises. Seven hundred years later, in June 2008, his sentence was revoked by Florence's city council.

Dante received his education in various places and sought knowledge among various traditions: Aristotelian, Platonic, Muslim, and especially the works of Thomas Aquinas and Catholicism.[1] He became one of the learned men of his time. In his early work and writings he was influenced by Guido Cavalcanti, who had been influenced by Aristotle. Cavalcanti was not only a poet but also knowledgeable in natural philosophy. In his *Donna Mi Prega*, Cavalcanti strove to describe the experience of love in strict philosophical terms.

Dante gradually moved away from a rationalistic view of love and instead emphasized the difference between knowledge of life and the experience of love. His inquiring mind led Dante to embark on a pilgrimage for truth. Philosophy and theology were the paths through which he acknowledged love as the highest form of the intelligence that created the world. At the same time, through love, Dante says, we can come to self-realization. The experience of love can reveal the hierarchy of forces that govern creation and enables the human mind and heart to participate in the divine light of intelligence. In Dante's later works, God is the center of reality and the way to understand all things created: their "truth" can be revealed through their relationship to God. A person who insists on regarding himself as the center of creation denies his own fundamental nature and rejects his own deepest reality. To know God and to know yourself are part of the same axis.

Apart from Dante's significance as a poet and philosopher, he was the first to use the Tuscan vernacular in serious writing. By using the vernacular rather than Latin, Dante proved his commitment to increasing understanding among common people, encouraging them to seek greater understanding of themselves.

The Divine Comedy

It was during his exile that Dante composed *The Divine Comedy*. Its original title, "The Comedy", suggests that it was a story with a happy ending. Only after Dante's death was "Divine" added to the title.

Although our concern here is with the personal development that takes place in part two of *The Divine Comedy*, in *Purgatory*, a brief comment on the entire work is certainly appropriate. *The Divine Comedy* can be studied from various disciplines, including theology, philosophy, linguistics and literary studies. It is mainly concerned with the ultimate, eternal destiny of the human soul. It is the mystical dimension of the work and its focus on life as a psycho-spiritual journey that has relevance for us.

The Divine Comedy is an epic poem that describes an imaginative journey told by Dante in the first person. It is an allegory in which persons, events and objects have literal as well as figurative meaning. For instance, Beatrice is a person, the most beloved woman, and a representation of the supernatural truth Dante was seeking to find. The Roman poet Vergilius Maro (70–19 BC), Virgil, his guide, likewise has symbolic meaning, e.g. that of human reason and will. The poem is written in a three-line rhyme form that Dante devised, called terza rima, although many translations do not retain this rhyme scheme. This is from the opening[2] of *The Divine Comedy*:

> In the midway of this our mortal life,
> I found me in a gloomy wood, astray
> Gone from the path direct: and e'en to tell
> It were no easy task, how savage wild
> That forest, how robust and rough its growth,
> Which to remember only, my dismay
> Renews, in bitterness not far from death.

It is a journey through the *Inferno, Purgatory and Paradise*. In this journey Dante moves from the lowest level to the uppermost one, from Hell to Heaven, accompanied and guided first by Virgil, who follows him through Hell and up through Purgatory, and then by Beatrice, who had sent Virgil in the first place and who follows Dante from the top of Mount Purgatory into Heaven. The journey examines the individual human heart.

At the outset Dante is asleep and lost in a dark wood. But he wants to move on and looks up. There he sees a beautiful mountain and sets out to climb it. He is stopped by three animals: a leopard, a lion and a female wolf – by his love of pleasure, by his fierce pride and by the terrifying greed and avarice of the ego. Fleeing back to the wood, he encounters Virgil, who tells him he cannot hope to reach the mountain that way. Instead, the only way for Dante is to trust in Virgil and follow him through Hell and Purgatory.

Psychologically, Dante's awakening in the dark wood can be seen as his looking within himself and finding there the capacity for evil, or the possibility of passively consenting to it. *The Inferno* can be read as an account of how weaknesses take over and determine a person's life. What is at first an innocent indulgence or failure to make the right choices gradually amounts to ultimate treachery. At the bottom of the pit, where the heart is hardened by loss of feeling and cut off from every bond of loyalty in perpetual frozenness, Satan himself is upside down. The way down then turns and becomes the way up. It is perhaps paradoxical that through the encounter with this evil the turn is made. Facing and becoming fully aware of the potential evil within means a turn to truth; down becomes up, towards the light.

At the summit of Purgatory it is Beatrice who explains to Dante that his inability to grasp the mysteries she present to him is caused by the school he has followed, meaning his training in philosophy, whose teachings are separate from God. Yet again these very teachings enable Dante to define with such doctrinal precision the passages that his soul undergoes. The danger is that rational and intellectual pride distance a person from knowing the truth that lies in experience, without which no change can occur. It is the transformative power of the direct experience of God that leads Dante to awakening. Throughout, Dante encounters his choices in the struggle between the outer form of knowledge, "The Church", either as Catholicism or intellectualism, and his commitment to his inner religion, the formless, mystical experience that at once illuminates everything thinking form can conceive.

From a psycho-spiritual viewpoint, the Inferno can be said to represent a state of being in which a person is a victim of the unknown or unacknowledged parts of his or her own personality, blaming others for the suffering this brings, and hence having no power to change it. In Purgatory, on the other hand, these same aspects of the personality are recognized, consciously suffered, and taken responsibility for. This way the personality is cleansed of unwanted aspects, purified of weaknesses, and slowly freed from the grip of ego limitations. Finally, in Paradise, the mind and heart are free to receive inspiration from the Divine source independent of personal and ego limitations.

Purgatory

Purgatory may be the least studied part of Dante's trilogy. It is not as horrible as the *Inferno* and not as beautiful as *Paradise*. It is in *Purgatory* that Dante's journey takes him past the seven sins and virtues that are of interest for our discussion. Purgatory differs from Hell and Heaven in that it teaches us the meaning of time. Both Hell and Heaven are eternal, timeless places. In Purgatory we are constantly reminded of how time and rhythm are what take us out of our limitations. Moreover, Purgatory requires patience and obedience to the laws of time.

Dante's Purgatory is a mountain surrounded only by the sea. It is inhabited by those who do penance after death to expiate their sins on Earth. At the bottom is ante-Purgatory, where the souls wander whose repentance has been delayed both in life and now in death. Above that is Purgatory proper, the place of active purgation. It consists of seven terraces, one above the other, connected by stairs in the rock. On each of these levels one of the seven sins is purged by the souls who were beset by them. At the top of the mountain is the Earthly Paradise, the Garden of Eden, from which the cleansed souls ascend to Heaven. Dante and Virgil arrive on Easter Sunday, the day celebrated in Christianity as the day when Jesus Christ was resurrected from the dead. They start their journey at sunrise.

At Peter's Gate, leading into Purgatory, three colors shine: white, black and red. The colors represent the three attitudes necessary for entering the gate. White symbolizes confession, the power to look within and see oneself as one is and to admit, accept and confess to whatever that might be. Black represents mourning, contrition, the regret that comes with full acceptance. Red, the color of blood, stands for pouring out love and life in restitution, which leads to satisfaction and is liberation.

The gate of Purgatory is guarded by an angel, who, with a sword, draws seven Ps on Dante's forehead. P stands for *peccatum*, which is Italian for "sin", and the angel asks of Dante that he now wash these inner stains away. At the same time Dante is not allowed to look back, but must leave behind his previous habits. To open the door, the angel uses two keys, one of silver and one of gold. They symbolize remorse and reconciliation, respectively, a combination necessary for forgiveness.

Souls who follow the rules of Purgatory can only move upwards, there is no going back, as the journey up the mountain is meant to lead to God. The souls are permitted to progress to the next level at any time. But there is a code of honor that prevents any soul from leaving before having corrected the weakness within that caused the wound which led to the sin. Purgatory not only requires patience, it fosters it.

Walking, or moving forward on the mountain of Purgatory, is only permitted in daylight. The light of God is the only true guide. Night is used for reflection, contemplation, dreams – all those things that belong to the realm of the unconscious and therefore do not count in the light of day. According to Helen Luke,[3] pausing in this state of being receptive or passive or listening is essential, and if it is not observed, then nothing stemming from this dimension can ever be consciously integrated, and no personal development or awareness can take place. We learn to deal with sin and virtue by understanding how much they hold us in their sway and consequently how much power they have over us. Only then can we become aware of how to avoid personally engaging in the dynamics between sin and virtue.

Purgatory is divided in three parts, representing three different ways of approaching love in the wrong way. The first three levels expiate "love perverted" or "love of neighbors' harm": pride, envy and anger. The three upper terraces deal with "excessive love of secondary objects":

greed, gluttony and lust. The sin in the middle, the fourth sin, represents "love defective": sloth.

An angel is stationed at the end of the curve of each level, who erases one "P" from Dante's forehead with his wing and makes the remaining "P"s fainter. This lightens Dante's burden and makes the rest easier.

Sins and virtues

Sin, in Dante's definition, is a denial, indifference to or excess of love. Each sin has a contrasting virtue, an attitude that can remedy the sin. It is formed by the qualities opposing the forces of the sin and superseding them. The virtue is the antidote, as it were, to sin, but does not replace it.

There is no punishment in Dante's Purgatory, no externally applied force that punishes souls for being stuck. Being stuck in the sin or the virtue is in itself the punishment. This is what it is all about: becoming free from what you have acquired psychologically and spiritually and which holds you in the grip of duality. Thus it is clear that a sin can quickly become a virtue and the other way around. What is seen as good at one period in time is seen as bad in another; the one is always regulated by the other. The virtue will not cure the sin, it just balances it. According to Dante, the way through Purgatory teaches a person to deal with these fundamental opposites. But how?

The souls in Purgatory receive a meditation consisting of an example of the sin and the virtue. This way these aspects become differentiated and the difference becomes clear to the soul. They also receive a prayer, emphasizing the selflessness by which the sin must be countered. When the purification is completed, the guardian angel of a virtue recites the relevant benediction and receives the soul, ready for the next trial. The angel of humility receives the proud; the angel of generosity the envious; the angel of gentleness the angry; the angel of zeal the slothful; the angel of charity the greedy; the angel of temperance the gluttonous; and the angel of chastity receives the lustful.

The seven sins and virtues are expressions of fundamental inclinations by which life is approached. It is not any specific behavior or deed that forms a sin, but the attitude and stain left as marks on the soul from having held that attitude. How do you manage yourself in relation to others, how do you value others in relation to yourself, what do you take and what do you give?

Duality, time, willingness to engage consciously with personal limitations, and responsibility for individual wounds are all part of the process that takes place on Mount Purgatory and leads to transformation.

From a psycho-spiritual viewpoint, this transformation process is equal to individuation, to becoming a full human being. Hardly anyone moves straight from being caught in unconscious indulgences to freedom from suffering and wholeness. There is always labor involved and a gradual release of inadequate habits of mind and behavior. Self-realization is an ongoing process.

The nature of the labor requires continuous attention. Every moment of our lives we have the opportunity to pay attention to how we approach the circumstances we find ourselves in. Self-pity is a habit of mind that cannot endure in this process; it simply does not lead forward. Instead, it is accepting that, as the wrathful say when blinded by the smoke of their anger, "if we can't see, at least we can hear," that accomplishes something with respect to others, without considering personal limitations. We learn to make the most of what is possible at any given time. And this attitude leads to another: objective courtesy.[4] This transformation means that an attitude is developed that considers what *is* – for the sake of life, yourself and the other.

From the perspective of analytical psychology, analysis is not very different from Dante's Purgatory. In fact what Dante describes is very well recognized as immediate fact by anyone involved in analysis. Because the terminology is different, some clarification of the relationship is called for.

Like Dante, Jung talks about confession as essential for the onset of analytical work. Confession, in Jung's view, is the first step towards acknowledging unwanted aspects of the personality.[5] You suffer from something, but you do not hide that from yourself any longer, so then you can also tell another person about it. You can start to seek help. Just as Dante was ready to accept and fully trust his guide Virgil, so we can today seek a confidant, someone we can trust and work with. Those who do not "confess" and thus do not allow themselves to be helped become stuck in what they already have.

More important than the particular training or tradition the helper draws on is to follow a single tradition. A blend of elements chosen from different sources – a little bit of Zen, some foot reflexology, an aura reading, and so on – a compilation of borrowed bits, will never work. You need to follow one line, one person who knows what he or she is doing; then you can have as much of "the little bits" as you want. The reason is that the bond between you and the person you choose makes the difference.[6] Dante was pushed through Hell and dragged up the Mountain of Purgatory by Virgil. He would never have made it on his own because it is not possible to retain hope when all is hopeless. Someone has to keep it for you. Only then is it possible and tolerable to enter that experience of deepest despair that will set you free. It would not be safe nor wise to venture this alone.

Instead of sins and virtues, contemporary psychology talks about autonomous complexes, narcissistic wounding, inflation, character structure and disorders, repetitive patterns of behavior, and the like. These are powers that influence the psyche and have the same effect on the person affected as do Dante's sins. You know you are caught in a complex[7] when you find yourself reacting out of all proportion at the slightest provocation, and reacting in a particular way, the same way you always react in similar situations, and you cannot stop it once it has started. It can be a reaction to what you perceive as unjust, unfair, authoritarian persons or an over-demanding boss. Finding out what triggers your autonomous reaction often helps you gradually loosen its grip so that you can become conscious of the old habits. You are then freer to choose your reaction.

Often people who once had an authority complex expressed in anger or rage become temporarily docile to an almost astonishing degree. This may be a compensating reaction, which indeed balances the personality and eventually leads to peace. Cleansing the "stains", the remains of habits and ways of relating, is part of the transformation that analysis facilitates. It does so by mellowing defense mechanisms such as denial (avoiding knowledge of what is perceived as negative in oneself or in the outside world) and projection (transposing unconscious weaknesses in oneself on to others). The transformation is concerned with everything that hinders regret, confession, differentiation, integration and your own approval of the new level in yourself from which you are free to act and progress.

Psychic reality is made up of various components, each having its own dynamics. Relevant to these[8] are the persona, the face a person uses when meeting the external world, which is used relatively consciously. Behind this mask, and largely unconscious, is the shadow, which is either our undeveloped qualities or our unwanted side – the denied "sins" of which one is unconscious – but often it can also contain positive, disowned personal qualities. A person encounters the external world with the persona and encounters the internal world with the animus in women and the anima in men. These can either be positive or negative. For a woman, a positive animus brings spirituality, self-acceptance and freedom to be in the world as she is. A negative animus, on the other hand, makes a woman controlling, self-critical, judgmental, possessive, argumentative, always wanting to have the last word. For a man the positive anima is the "she" within him, his connection with his soul. A negative anima makes men whining, complaining, sentimental and powerless.

For Dante, the positive anima is embodied by Beatrice. She is the inner guide who takes Dante to his soul's goal, the White Rose, and she was the one who sent Virgil to care for Dante.

In my observation, a major impulse to awakening the positive anima and animus and to platonic love, which may eventually lead to self-realization, occurs around the age of seven to ten years, in pre-puberty.[9] Then the image of that inner figure is formed, often influenced by the parent of the opposite sex, as a result of his or her presence and special contact with the child, or by his or her absence and lack of contact. Once more, in Dante's life the latter was the case. His mother died when he was about nine years old, close to the time when he first saw Beatrice. It may be speculation, but perhaps Dante found in the beautiful Beatrice all the qualities he had hoped his mother would transmit, qualities such as self-sacrificing love, encouragement and spiritual education. In any case, meeting Beatrice was an encounter that cut through and awakened a new intensity of feeling *inside* Dante.

For example, in women leaders today the positive animus has some traits in common with the Dante that journeys through Purgatory. He has qualities of passion, endurance, intelligence, truth-seeking and commitment to an ideal, to personal development. Women I have worked with often talk about a particular moment around the age of six to nine with their father, teacher, or an idol, or another encounter, that surged through their whole being and transformed the experience of what being alive meant. This made such an impression that later in life their partner shows traits similar to this earlier person. It may be an oversimplification to say that women seek husbands who resemble their father. The point here is that if a woman has had that special, significant encounter which formed the external image of her inner ideal, then that will be what she needs as an inner beacon to thrive and feel relaxed. For a man, embracing his positive anima opens the door to gentleness, chivalry and truth seeking.

Relevance for feminine leadership

Leaders I work with have done what Dante did. They have chosen to wake up and have a look around, assemble their courage, and enter the journey that leads through their inner landscape, which has been formed by upbringing and life experiences, and to start to map that geography, creating consciousness and liberation from its pitfalls. They report that among the benefits of all the effort that goes into such a process are compassion for themselves and others, a balance between activity and repose, and a conscious use of timing. Because they are less entrenched in their own objectives, they can more easily discern when the right moment has come for any activity or decision, and what is very important, to respond to it adequately. Let us be honest: sometimes we know that something is overdue or premature, but because our own motives may be entangled (such as fear or some kind of investment), we are unable to act effectively.

Moreover, what they report as a great benefit is the access they get to a form of creative intelligence not based on rationality. Perhaps it is intuition or creativity; in any case, what it does is present entirely new ways of perceiving a situation. It is like seeing the world with new eyes. Again, to get the full benefit of course a person needs to have the courage to accept the consequences of this new perspective, which is not always easy. It might mean that a person must go against a majority of shareholder interests or act against a social code or collegial expectations. Yet we can all think of instances when leaders have been so infatuated with their own inspiration that reckless decisions were made, and their creativity led to much suffering. This negative use of inspiration is often found in people who have not suffered from their wounds and healed them, or those who have not yet entered Purgatory. The process of Purgatory fosters the judgment necessary for unselfish use of the creative intelligence: of the love that has the power of creation.

Earlier we noted that the development of the positive anima and animus is essential for any leadership. Apart from keeping a person company, as it were, because at times it is lonely, the positive animus or anima becomes the voice of conscience. Not in a moralistic way, but rather in preventing the takeover of self-delusion, because honesty becomes much more important than how it "should" be. The positive anima and animus becomes more conscious, closer, visible through dreamwork. By noting down the dreams you have at night, perhaps keeping a dream log, studying your dreams and starting to understand the symbolic language, you may discover the nature of your positive animus/anima and start to interact with it. To further emphasize that inner connection active imagination, which is a technique for visualizing dialogue, may be applied. Once you start moving towards such an "inner marriage", your outer partnerships will not only prosper but take on completely new, more fulfilling qualities.

Then, finally, there is that place of grace, the eye of the storm, the central resting point within yourself that feels like being at home with yourself – the point that somehow holds together your whole universe, the place from which the various demands that life provides in the form of marriage, children, work, friendship, and all forms of activities pertaining to the outer life, as well as your dreams, hopes and fears, are coordinated with all of yourself fully present. Coming to that place requires training and experience;[10] that is, meditation, breathing practices and teachings in a given tradition. From my own personal experience of being guided and serving as a guide in Sufism and as a psychoanalyst, I have come to believe that when this level of exchange occurs, all important messages are transmitted non-verbally and through other means of communication than the ones we ordinarily acknowledge as such. I think of a moment of meeting[11] that may perhaps consist of a glance, a word or a silent moment together, when all that is available is available at once. For very obvious reasons it is difficult to formulate precisely the intensity of such moments. Nevertheless, this is evidence that mysticism, the pursuit of experiential knowledge of unity in creation,[12] is applicable just as much today as it has always been.

Notes

1 Dante studied the works of Aristotle that were available in Latin at the time. Thomas Aquinas' work incorporates Aristotelian teachings into Catholic theology.

2 Alighieri, D. *The Divine Comedy I: Hell*, Canto I: 1, Gutenberg publication: 2004. Translation by the Rev. H.F. Cary, M.A. Urbana, IL: Project Gutenberg. Retrieved 5 June 2019 from www.gutenberg.org/ebooks/8789.

3 Luke, H. (1989). *Dark Wood to White Rose: Journey and Transformation in Dante's Divine Comedy*. New York: Parabola.

4 See Luke (1989), pp. 54–55.

5 In the analytical process, confession is followed by elucidation, education and transformation.

6 For different perspectives on the analytical relation, transference and countertransference, see, for example, Sedgwick, D. (2005). *The Wounded Healer: Countertransference from a Jungian Perspective*. London: Routledge; Samuels, A. (2006). Transference/countertransference. In *The Handbook of Jungian Psychology*, edited by Papadopoulos, R. London: Routledge; and Guggenbühl-Craig, A. (1971). *Power in the Helping Profession*. Putnam, CT: Spring Publications.

7 See Jacobi, J. (1959). *Complex, Archetype, Symbol in the Psychology of C.G. Jung*. London: Routledge & Kegan Paul.

8 Commonly recognized in analytical psychology. For references, see Samuels, A., Shorter, B. and Plaut, F. (1986). *A Critical Dictionary of Jungian Analysis*. London: Routledge.

9 Or "latency period" in Freudian terminology.

10 Probably people with near-death experiences, for instance, will contest this. My point here is merely that following mystical training is a conscious

choice to develop your self in a certain direction, which allows you to experience your self from a fuller, freer, and more unified vantage point.

11 "Moment of meeting" is a "now moment" that is part of therapy or coaching. It is the process of non-verbal interaction that is full of portent and meaning and responded to authentically by both parties as they progress. See Hogenson (2009), p. 189.

12 Mysticism is the pursuit of communion with (unity) or conscious awareness (presence) of an ultimate reality through direct experience. See, for example, Hood, Hill and Spilka (2009), pp. 333, 337.

Chapter 3

Pride and humility

Pride and humility have their roles to play in Western society. More often than not captains of industry have until recently displayed signs of overt pride rather than humility. And they have been feared, followed and admired for it, to the point that pride has in fact become an indication of how a real leader can be recognized. Leadership development programs, on the other hand, do not emphasize this trait, but rather foster humble cooperation. This is typical of our ambivalence about pride.

There is a saying in Dutch, "Je hoofd niet boven het maaiveld uit-steken," which means "Don't stand out." In this way the Dutch caution against holding your head too high above others or trying to be above average. The advice is to remember that you are not special or better than anyone else. It is so widespread that anyone deliberately showing off cannot help being aware of the risk of correction, sooner or later. Since this is so central to the national persona, the Netherlands is most likely to host a shadow composed of lavishness, extraordinary individualism and self-centeredness; in short, many very un-Calvinistic traits and attitudes. The opposites of prudence and extravagance became visible in the 1990s when the baby boom generation introduced a level of luxury and consumption previously unheard of in Dutch society, which was signified by a willingness to spend money to show off.

Whether excelling is regarded with reservation or kept as a hidden dream, the Dutch excel in many areas, even on a global scale. Characteristic for Dutch excellence is that it occurs within the framework of the collective and often for the collective – the introduction of joint stock companies, for instance, allowed shareholders to invest in business ventures and obtain a share of their profits and losses. Or take the example of strategies for saving the country from the sea, which were developed by farmers and nobles who, possibly forced by nature, jointly formed unified defenses against the sea and so laid the grounds for the polder model, a consensus policy for decision-making characteristic of Dutch leadership and democracy. The Dutch may be proud of their humble service to the common interest. In a way their approach reconciles pride and humility in practice. To be proud of that is to be content with doing the right thing, and that is legitimate. It must not be confused with the problematic pride we seek to understand here, which by contrast prompts people to seek to enhance their own condition, position and benefit, not seldom at the expense of others.

But then again is there not, even in the Netherlands, something attractive about the pride that exceeds the collective and stands out as superior? Do we not admire, even if just a little, the extraordinary, the mighty, the proud? And are we not sometimes repulsed, even if just a little, by pathetic, weak humility? And does humility not at times seem vainer than vain? Yes, even among us the shadow has an attraction, because it wants to be integrated rather than pushed away. Somehow we know it is undifferentiated and unintegrated pride that leads to outer forms of domination, such as racism and "holy" wars, as well as more local domestic expressions. We also intuitively know that, albeit in its collective manifestations, such integration can occur only through individual effort.

For leaders the risk of blindly falling into pride is isolation, ruin and torment. They will have no rest, but feel permanently driven to win over others and prove themselves superior. They will be aggressive without noticing themselves. Because of their competitiveness, nobody will trust them. If people avoid them or try to work around them, this will increase aggressive outbursts and accelerate competitiveness. This will be their life at work, at home, at the hockey club or on the tennis court, and even in their most intimate moments.

There are the obvious gains ensuing from consciously engaging with pride and exploring what power pride desires to mimic. Acknowledging that pride does not further these gains is the most important step towards dissolving its grip. Dante teaches us that pride is a burden.

Pride and humility in Dante's *Purgatory of the Divine Comedy*

Pride (*Superbia*) is the sin at the bottom of lower Purgatory. The description reads, "love of self perverted to hatred and contempt for one's neighbor." Pride is the first of the seven major sins and considered the root of all sins. It is the desire to be more important, to be above everyone else, and it is an individual's desire to be in control of his or her own life and dominate the lives of others. In its wider perspective, pride is understood as driving all subsequent sins because it aims to equate man with God. When pride operates in a person, he or she is driven to seek a central position at all costs. This can look like egotism, vanity and self-centeredness, but at bottom it represents a personality in constant competition with everyone and everything. For the proud there is no rest from the drive to shine, to prove what that inner voice relentlessly repeats: you are the one.

In Purgatory this is illustrated by the proud willingly carrying heavy stones on their necks and backs, making them walk on their knees, unable to look up. In atonement for their pride, which made them place themselves above all others, they are now close to the ground. They are burdened down by the weight of all that they wanted to control and have power over. Pride does not tolerate being countered and most fears humiliation. Losing face in the company of others, any sign of vulnerability or the slightest inkling of falling behind, being passed, anything small, fuels the rage that is always alive and burning night and day in the proud. To humiliate a proud person is a real risk. It is therefore interesting that it is *humility* that is the virtue that may release a person from the grip of pride. Yet again, in Purgatory it is the encounter or confrontation with sin that releases it.

In Purgatory the proud ones learn about their pride through prayer, especially the prayer to Our Father, the *Paternoster*. The prayer is taken to a state of contemplation where special attention is given to each passage of the prayer. The second phrase reads:

> May thy kingdom's peace
> Come unto us; for we, unless it come,
> With all our striving thither tend in vain.[1]

The proud are redeemed by acknowledging that inner peace cannot be obtained merely through their own initiative and willpower. They admit they cannot command their different states or the reach of their influence, but must depend on something greater than themselves. When they acknowledge this, it brings about a form of humility, which is experienced as a relief: there is nothing humiliating about being human.

Humility, unlike pride, is the ability to see and feel that another person is just as important, valuable and beautiful as you are. It is recognizing the value of another race or person's achievements, whether totally different from yours or in competition with yours.

Humility is more than mere cognition of fairness of judgment or equality. Dorothy L. Sayers establishes that to fully grasp that special shimmering quality of humility, which is such a neglected quality in today's society, it is important to look at Beatrice's effect on Dante. Beatrice induces Dante's willing submission because he trusts her. Perhaps in his heart he knows that it was she who sought him? He sees in her luminous being a beacon for his soul's self-realization. Humility is the quality of graceful surrender. It is peace, sweetness, softness, delight, suspension of the heart, serenity. When he passed the final test of pride, Dante asked Virgil:

> Master, what heavy load
> Has slipped from me, so that I walk with ease,
> And scarcely feel fatigue upon the road?

From the moment pride is overcome, the steps are lighter and the mountain easier to climb. With the pardon of pride, the conquest of the rest is easier. Dante emphasizes the freedom and lightness he feels when the "P" of Pride has been erased. Dante's intuition and imagination can be affirmed by psychology, which in turn looks further into its roots and causes and suggests methods for relieving a person of this burden, making living lighter.

Personal developmental aspects of pride and humility

The idea, and sometimes secret conviction, that there is something that makes you more special than anyone else is of course a recognizable trait. We all have moments when identification with the unique in us takes over and we forget traits that we share with others. Then we normally fall back, or something happens that reminds us that we are not all that special. It is not such occasional fluctuations that we look for here, but the much deeper pattern that can sometimes govern a person's whole life and development.

Modern psychology is concerned with defining traits that seem to cluster together and so form a certain pattern of self-image, feeling, cognition and behavior. We all have these traits, which are the building blocks of our personality, and are known from antiquity and earlier.[2] In that sense this is all normal. When certain patterns become the prevailing and only way of living, however, a person may start to suffer. That person might start to feel it is not really himself or herself, that is to say, it is not how I know myself in essence. The purpose of psychology's attempts to diagnose is to apply adequate methods for helping a person overcome such patterns when they start to hinder his or her life.

One diagnosis frequently revisited in psychoanalytical practice that comes close to Dante's pride is called narcissism. There are different forms and degrees of this. Just as pride in a way is the basis for subsequent sins, it is possible to say that narcissism, in all its varieties, is prevalent in most people's psychological makeup, especially among Westerners. The myth of Narcissus can serve as the embodiment of the form of narcissism known as alpha-narcissism,[3] which is relevant in relation to pride.

Narcissus was a beautiful young boy who was adored by many but never reciprocated the love and adulation he received. Narcissus was self-absorbed and felt he was impervious to the arrows of Amor. The Nymph Echo, who at this point in the drama is limited to echoing the voice of others (because before she used to speak all the time), was smitten by him and followed him in the fairy woods to implore his love. But alas, Narcissus was not available. As she lovingly caressed him, he asked that she take her hands off him:

> Thus rejected, she lies hidden in the deep woods, hiding her blushing face with green leaves; and ever after lives concealed in lonely caverns in the hills. But her great love increases with neglect; her miserable body wastes away, wakeful with sorrows; leanness shrivels up her skin, and all her lovely features melt, as if dissolved upon the wafting winds – nothing remains except her bones and voice – her voice continues in the wilderness; her bones have turned to stone.[4]

Now, for Narcissus this was not a unique event, but was his habitual way of responding to approaches. Once a despised youth from the depth of his suffering cried out to the gods that if Narcissus should fall in love, they should deny him what he loved. Nemesis heard the prayer and granted it. Thus, in punishing Narcissus for his lack of humility, empathy, and any form of reaching out to his admirers, the gods made him fall in love with his own reflection in a pool. "What he sees is nothing in itself." Narcissus: "I must love and behold; yet what I see and love, I cannot reach: so powerful is the illusion of my love."[5] When it dawned on him that he could not complete this love, that nothing was to be achieved in terms of relationship, he killed himself.

The myth of Echo and Narcissus has many dimensions, all equally noteworthy. The inclination that has been called "narcissism" is here illustrated by self-centeredness and indulgence in one's own sense of (physical, mental) greatness, lack of empathy for others, and rejection and scorning of the surrendering quality of love. Echo personifies the other side, the voice that lives without a body. It is a form of involuntary submission. Echo, in her thirst for touches and caresses, reaches out but is denied, and so dies from rejection. She is the wounded side and yet the one that goes on; in its despair her echo over the hills has an eternal quality.

If we look at the myth in its totality, and if Echo and Narcissus were to be regarded as one united entity, then we can see how narcissism works. It is the interplay of being rejected, abandoned and humiliated on the one hand, and rejecting, abandoning and humiliating on the other. The core can be defined as longing for a love that is experienced as impossible. This is what is significant for the narcissism we see here. It is the combination of being on top of the world (superior) and yet always on guard (helpless), with the relational pattern of rejecting in a distressed state of solitude. It has its roots in early childhood.

Imagine a child whose mother does not look at her or him often, or touch, talk to or lovingly hold them. The child has somehow received enough attention to develop a longing for loving contact, but not enough of that attention. The child knows what it feels but cannot get to feel it, or comes in contact with the feeling and then it is withdrawn or mixed up with something else such as aggression or sexuality. The child becomes confused and distrusting of loving relationships, which it starts to reject. Consequently, as this child grows up other mechanisms compensating for the abyss of emptiness will develop and be put into practice. Among the most common defense mechanisms are aggression and splitting.[6]

The abandonment that the child experiences creates a wound of the sort that will not heal by itself. Defenses are put in place not only to ward off others, but also as protection from contact with the hurt inside. With no real inner contact, dissociation from feelings and from the body follows. And with that lack of essential feedback from within yourself and what you perceive from the world around, all sorts of things become possible. Reckless decisions can be made without any alarm bells going off. Unpredictable and "unreal" or unethical communications frequently occur. People around this person often, consciously or not, feel alienated just as this person is alienated from themselves.

Leadership development through pride and humility

Pride is not uncommon among leaders. In fact, we have become so used to it that to a certain extent we also identify leadership through these qualities: independence, aggression, attraction, the "lone rider" who appears socially appropriate yet unavailable.

In leadership development, with pride and humility[7] as the entrance point and the levers for personal growth, it is critical to distinguish between outer behavior and inner feelings, because they are not congruent. A leader with pride at the core seeks nourishment by rejecting close contact with people. This is the paradox that when addressed and worked with in the analytical setting can lead to real compassion. That is the hidden and protected jewel at the heart of the matter. It is, however, not unproblematic to approach this gem, especially in the initial phase of development. Leaders with pride generally do not initially seek personal development in order to have more contact with humility. On the contrary, they often ask how to strengthen their pride, because they feel that for some reason their habitual style has started to collapse and they are falling behind.

Another visible manifestation of this form of pride in leaders, close to the competitiveness theme, is their wish for dominance. This does not include all forms of dominance, but is relevant for leaders who always want the final say or steer everyone else according to their will – overt ways of dominating people and situations. Another relevant form of dominance is the one that others observe through these leaders' control of all minute details, their almost eerie "knowledge" about people's locations, ideas, moves, conversations, and their intricate way of being involved in all this and remembering things for a very long time.

In essence, this particular form of dominance relates to the desire, sometimes compulsion, to dominate the Self, the spiritual spark within, the soul, the life force, the personality – all things that we are made of, without ever having consented to or revoked them – so that by ruling these, all else will be governed. Such dominance excludes any form of "letting go". Letting go of impulses, bodily expressions or mind control threatens the anchor that this form of dominance provides the leader in question. Teetotalism and compulsively engaging in sports are but a few forms of this dominance. For leaders captive to this aspect of pride, oversleeping is about the lowest they allow themselves "to sink".

For leaders with this drive it can help to find a goal outside themselves to focus all that discipline, structure and fine eye for detail. When they willingly and successfully orient themselves towards non-material or non-obtainable ends, anything related to process rather than goal, they can experience tremendous benefits. I have witnessed more than one developing quickly through meditation that gives momentary release from that constant drive. Any regular practice geared towards stilling the mind and allowing what is to be seems to help the process of slowly allowing for the autonomous side of life that lives, whether we control it or not. Joint exploration of the sensation of living invites a broader and more accepting perspective on the nature of living. It introduces the notion of trust and a consideration of the possibility that things can happen and go well at work when such a person is not on top of it all.

Leaders who seek personal development because of their pride often enter analysis with a communication issue. They experienced themselves as verbally abusive at times and want to look for new ways of interacting. Inquiry into their habitual way of interacting and communicating often reveals a back-and-forth pattern. There can, for instance, have been a sudden fallout with a close and devoted assistant, who in their own eyes has done nothing to deserve such treatment. Then again, if the slightest form of accusation, a simple question even, is asked of this proud person, they will immediately feel very hurt and often react fearfully, going into retreat or regression. The back and forth is between being all powerful and being nothing. Too much self-worth or too much self-loathing produces these radical swings, and the tension between such extremes brings much suffering. It is as if the one undoes the other, leading to a feeling of emptiness, of living nothingness and powerlessness. Looking beyond the actual communication exchange often leads to the subjectively felt lack of balance. These leaders say they feel as if they are not stable, as if there is no solid ground under their feet. One client expressed it as follows:

> I am always a little bit anxious and I have my anxiety to thank for a lot – it has driven me to great achievements – but now I feel it starts to empty me of energy, and I know I cannot go on in the same way as before. I want to be more relaxed in life, but then again that feels like a risk, and as soon as I feel that, it swings back again and I am on the ball again. It is like constantly balancing on a ball, while knowing that you actually don't know how to balance. So you know you will fall, it is just a matter of time.

We both "knew" that the only true response to such a state would be one in which I would be holding, create space for safety, stability, groundedness and togetherness with me. But, given that the need for this was so sensitive and paired with such a feeling of disgust, neither of us could really move into such mental holding, let alone express the need for it verbally. Yet, we practiced it, and it proved superior in a new way. Gradually my client got the upper hand over pride and could allow empathy and affection for the wounded aspect of the personality to heal it.

That leads us to the most insufferable place of pride: nurturing relationships, which at the same time is its remedy. More than anyone else, the proud person may learn to enjoy being held until the connection within the Self is established. This does indeed require humility. Having said that, we need to explain how humility serves the proud. As we have seen earlier, pride and humility are two sides of the same coin, one holds the potential of the other. But pride is not the only one of these two that is one-sided. When humility becomes too excessive, we see examples of false humility. A familiar such image is the "servant leaders" who claim no needs of their own, a kind of Dickensian character, "'Umble we are, 'umble we have been, 'umble we shall ever be,"[8] refusing any favor at all, yet often manipulating in the background. To overcome pride, it will not help to engage in such excessive humility, however common such attempts might be. We instinctively know this, and that is perhaps the major reason why we react by finding this kind of humility vainer than vain. We somehow know it is insincere and an empty defense against the suffering of having needs and feeling unworthy. For the sake of development, we do not want to let that happen.

The characteristic of humility that can help overcome or at least loosen the grip of pride is that aspect of it that cannot be claimed. It might seem a paradox – to embrace a trait that cannot be claimed. Yet it is true for reasons of self-worth. Intrinsic self-worth is invisible and non-material – a thing that for the proud needs careful cultivation because true self-worth is the power that pride mimics. If you can feel yourself to be a truly valuable person independent of the worth you ascribe to others, and if you do not feel threatened by others no matter how valuable they seem to you, then you have the ability not only to see but to value others as yourself. And then you can really start to become creative. All that force that had been locked in aggression and competition is freed to be unleashed in any business of your choice.[9] Transforming pride into good for others, and surrender to a cause is as heroic as its potential outcome in practice. Dante's humility comes from a safe place. Recalling how the encounter with Beatrice taught him humility he declares:

> Therefore, when love so deprives me of power that my spirits seem to desert me, my frail soul tastes such sweetness that my cheeks grow pale. Then my sighs beseech my lady to grant me further salute. This happens every time she looks upon me, and is a thing so *umil* [humbling] that it passes belief.[10]

Contrary to Narcissus and Echo, Dante and Beatrice have no problem giving in to each other, to the soul's longing for peace and beauty. The inner woman knows this place of peace and tranquility, which Beatrice radiates: "She bore about her so true an *umiltà* [humility], that she seemed to say, I am at peace."[11] One benefit of having worked on humility in your leadership development is that you know its terrain, whether in the form of peace, kindness, compassion or any other form of appreciation for the other. This is authentic humility. Your own value as a person brings about the "me feeling" that is safe and peaceful. It is nobody else's business.

Leadership and submission may seem like a paradoxical pair. Yet attaching to a leader who radiates a felt sense of self-worth is not difficult – on the contrary, as we know, it feels natural, good and safe. Their natural inclination to loyalty is directed to a higher cause, one for which they may fight courageously and compassionately. Free submission emanates from and generates true leadership.

Reflections on humility

Esther Talboom

When I was 29 I had a near-death experience. I had given birth to our daughter at home – as a doctor, I thought I should be capable of doing so. All went well and the midwife had left, when I went to the toilet and started bleeding profusely. Within seconds I collapsed to the floor, unable to move, let alone sit up or call for help. My husband found me unconscious, called for an ambulance and carried me to bed.

The paramedics arrived and reanimated me before taking me together with my newborn daughter to the hospital. In the emergency room, I received the best treatment you can imagine and I soon recovered. But it was a life-changing event. It impacted my entire outlook, tremendously enhanced my sensitivity – something I've had to work on understanding – and showed me that material reality is but a veil over the essence of life.

A formative career experience

My career started when I worked as a general practitioner in an underprivileged area in Rotterdam noted for its criminality, poverty and related social disadvantages. I was in a team of forty, consisting of doctors, nurses, pharmaceutics, psychologists, psychiatrists and a primary healthcare unit.

My choice to spend years in this environment was prompted by social motives. I wanted to change the widely held perception that those who need healthcare the most receive it last, or not at all. Before long I became the team coordinator and during the ten years I worked in Rotterdam, I experienced a sense of flow within the group. We worked together seamlessly and achieved what nobody could have accomplished by themselves. Members of the community came to trust in care far beyond cure.

The challenges I face today

I am currently CEO of an innovative diagnostic knowledge center called Saltro. We work directly with patients as well as healthcare professionals in large hospitals and with about 600 primary care centers, we are one the largest in the Netherlands.

When I started working here, employment satisfaction was at a record low. Many, perhaps most, felt disempowered, fearful and hostile.

I set out to change that by creating cross-disciplinary teams assigned to work together on short-term projects and create successful solutions to everyday problems. I also initiated different settings in which important conversations could be held, and made sure to always partake in these conversations myself. It opened up the culture, fostered fluid communication and brought people together, as well as building on self-confidence. After eight years, the company received the Best Employer of the Year Award. It was very rewarding for all of us and I'm prouder of that than the International Healthcare Innovation Award that I received in Dubai recently. Tech innovation comes from driven professionals, but organizational innovation requires the cooperation of all its members.

Why tech matters to health

Technology is key today; it drives innovation and has and will have an ever-bigger impact on the doctor/patient relationship. It will also continuously impact the vision around cures. For example, we will increasingly be moving towards preventive healthcare, grounded in a holistic vision in which the patient is treated, not the disease.

E-health allows for implementation of tailored applications. For instance, there is a huge diversity among the group of chronic patients and their healthcare needs vary accordingly. That's why I started a project in which I included lung patients in an effort to provide tailored treatment to each individual a decade ago.

Making the professional personal

I learned about this in a more in-depth fashion as I corresponded with individual patients by email. Some needed guidance for testing, support and advice on a bi-weekly basis, whereas for others, bi-annual contact sufficed. Having their voice heard increased their participation tremendously.

What I feel to be one of the most important findings of my PhD research is that most patients embrace, appreciate and benefit from tailored online healthcare. It's relevant because it's personal.

Lately I find myself in very profound conversations with general practitioners, academics, nurses, analysts and scientists who seek to understand how to manage the intense changes in their practice. And just as I function as an informal counselor in these conversations, I receive feedback, support and insights. I enjoy these shifts in my role so much.

My brand of feminine leadership

My leadership style is defined by real connection. I do not like being looked up to. It makes me feel insecure and somehow excluded. Instead I invest in close and frequent conversations with members of the different teams I work with.

When I encounter resistance to change, people who drag their feet and sabotage progress, I tend to invest in those who *do* work for renewal, improvement and positive developments. I find that it creates less tension in the group. Everybody knows where there is flow and it's only confusing if I spend too much time and energy on what's stagnated.

When leading disruptive innovation, per definition, one steps into the unknown. I try to balance the unrest with informed self-confidence, courage and trust in the process and in committed colleagues. And, most importantly, there are always angels in one form or the other who move it all forward.

Notes

1 Alighieri, D. (2004). *The Divine Comedy II: Purgatory*, Canto XI: 7. Translation by the Rev. H.F. Cary, M.A. Urbana, IL: Project Gutenberg. Retrieved 5 June 2019 from www.gutenberg.org/ebooks/8795.
2 Millon and Davis (1996), p. 226.
3 "The alpha narcissistic person experiences himself as able to make decisions and act on them. He feels able to take charge and frequently "win over" others that he feels he is stronger than, and he often identifies himself as a leader. He is acutely aware of his position in relationship to others, in groups, and is inclined to move to the head of the pack. He is not infrequently surprised when others describe him as aggressive. Establishing himself at the top of any pecking order serves to relieve anxiety and create an internal experience of safety" Dougherty and West (2007), p. 217.
4 Ovid. (1922). *Metamorphoses*, Book 3. Translation by Brookes More. Boston, MA: Cornhill, p. 370 ff.
5 Ovid. (1922). *Metamorphoses*, Book 3. Translation by Brookes More. Boston, MA: Cornhill, pp. 446–447.

6 See, for example, Jacobi, M. (1984). *The Analytical Encounter: Transference and Human Relationship*. Toronto: Inner City Books.
7 Uriah Heep, in *David Copperfield* (Dickens, 1994).
8 Alighieri, D. (1969). *La Vita Nouva*, XXVIII. Translation by Barbara Reynolds.
9 Holiday, R. (2014). *The Obstacle Is the Way: The Timeless Art of Turning Trials into Triumph*. New York: Portfolio.
10 Alighieri, D. (1969). *La Vita Nouva*, XXIII. Translation by Barbara Reynolds.
11 Alighieri, D. (1969). *La Vita Nouva*, XXIII. Translation by Barbara Reynolds.

Chapter 4

Envy and generosity

It has been said of envy that it is the most miserable sin because, unlike the other sins, nobody likes it, the envious person least of all. Envy is resentment and hostility towards someone because of something desirable that the person possesses. It is the tormenting drive to have that which someone else has. You notice that someone else has something that you do not have, and it upsets you greatly. As soon as you have acquired whatever it is and have that thing, you are still not happy. The drive has not abated because that is not the real issue. Envy generally is not about the object or the advantage that provokes the envy. What drives envy is the desire to access something of fundamental value: self-confidence, charm, beauty, popularity and other qualities of the Self. But instead of searching for such inner qualities, these are projected externally, and we might see them everywhere. Envy is not about ownership and material possession, but has a more existential character. That is why the desire has no bottom, no end to it.[1] We are not in contact with our own self-value when we are envious.

Envy manifests in many different forms. Most classic is to deprive the envied of something. Let us say you have had a difficult weekend and your partner has disappointed you, so you are hurt and unhappy, and feel ugly. Then on Monday morning you enter the office and see your colleague looking radiant. He laughs, flirts and describes the weekend with his new lover. You feel envy. Later that day, knowing that your colleague has invested substantially in a project he wants to become the owner of, you manipulate some people and processes that reflect very badly on your colleague, and his chance to become project owner is significantly reduced. You feel better. You were not interested in the project and did not want it yourself. Instead, your whole envy drive became geared towards taking it away from him and making him suffer. That way neither of you will be happy, and that reduces your own discomfort.

This makes envy a dark desire, dependent on the failure of the envied. It has been said that envy is ultimately the desire to destroy good and to experience satisfaction from doing so.[2] Because envy is not about a desire for an object or an advantage, but is rather rooted in an inner sense of deprivation, the envious person rarely tries to win the object that the envied has acquired but instead waits for misfortune to strike so that success is taken away from the envied. Envy-driven competition will not lead to expansion of potential but rather to deprivation of it.

Envy and generosity between groups can be rooted in comparisons between rich and poor, white or black, winners and losers. Similarly, envy between individuals at work is founded on performance, appreciation, perks, influence and other factors that indicate a person has value. We see divisions in such interrelated subgroups in offices, hospitals, educational institutions and in most other work environments. Western institutions that regulate these forces are tax systems and labor regulations. Envy at work is necessary because regulating deviance inhibits potentially dangerous differences between individuals and groups. One could perhaps say that envy tells people that they may not excel too much. At the same time it is also a threat to the business because it hinders productivity and innovation. Therefore, managing envy and generosity is indispensable. In particular, the fear of the consequences of envy must be managed to ensure stability and freedom. One common strategy for managing that fear is rationalization of inequalities among people. The purpose is to explain and so justify that some have more of a certain asset than others. In religion, the Roman Catholic Church is one of several institutions that rationalized fear of envy by saying that one should not envy another because what the other has and can do is the will of God. From this perspective, achievements, power and wealth are part of the will of God.

On a person-to-person basis, generosity, the virtue and counterpole of envy, is perhaps the most common approach against envy. By offering something to the envious, we quietly hope that they will back off and stop hating us for what we sometimes cannot help – in fact, we may try to hide it rather than vaunt it – but we nevertheless may attract envy. As we see in the *Cinderella* story, such generosity sometimes makes things worse.

Generosity can be a way of countering your own envy. When envy has become conscious and acceptable to you and you notice when it occurs, then your best way of countering the drive is to generously grant that person whatever happiness they seem to have. There are institutionalized forms for this too.

We may try to avoid envy, yet it has us all in its thrall. As long as we participate in society, interact, work, get a promotion, have relationships, raise children, seek schools and clubs for them, buy a car or a bike, book a holiday, buy groceries, we are subject to envy. Comparison is inescapable in Western society, which is based on capitalism that promotes competition. So, we can think differently and create mini-communities that are non-competitive, or behave as if we are unaffected by comparison. Still, competition remains an objective fact and is an unavoidable condition of life in the Netherlands and in most of the West, as well as in socialist countries that endorse envy of the ones who have much more. Let us not deny that we are immersed in comparisons and potential envy.

Despite the fact that it is such a widespread, almost universal, phenomenon, envy is very difficult to assess and even more difficult to understand through self-reports, because people rarely want to talk about their envy. This is probably because envy is such a negative emotion. To admit to envy is to openly declare that you are inferior to someone else and hostile to that person. Therefore, it is most often repressed or denied.

Envy is frequently rephrased and confused with jealousy, but these are quite different notions. Jealousy is a protective emotion against what is perceived as a threat to a valued relationship or to its quality. Jealousy spurs people to protect marriages and keep a specific social order, to hold on to what they have. Envy, by contrast, is a hostile feeling towards something desirable. Jealousy is a social notion and its value changes with time. Some decades ago, in the 1950s and 1960s, jealousy was generally seen as something positive. It was regarded as proof of togetherness and commitment, for example, the strength of the marriage. Subsequently, with increasing personal freedom in relationships, the meaning of jealousy was transformed. In the 1970s and 1980s it came to signal weakness and low self-esteem. Self-help movements offered assistance to people suffering directly from jealousy or from guilt over jealousy. Envy, on the other hand, can be distinguished by its permanent qualities, insensitive to race, creed and time.

Envy and generosity in Dante's Purgatory

Envy (*Invidia*) in Dante's definition is "love of one's own good perverted into a desire to deprive other men of theirs." Dante encounters the envious when reaching the second level in Purgatory. The envious sit there, leaning on the mountain, clad in grey haircloth and with their eyes sewn together with a steel wire. They are blind beggars, poverty incarnate, living on alms at the mercy of others' generosity.

Among the envious are two types: the ones who resent joy in other people, and the ones who take more joy in others' loss than in their own gain. Because of their neediness, the envious take themselves very seriously and do not assess comparison in the right proportions. Cain, who killed his brother Abel because his offering was accepted by God while Cain's was not, is among the lamenting envious.

Significant for envy is that it is rooted in fear. While the proud are self-sufficient and reject others, unable to see anyone as their equal or superior, the envious are always afraid that they are disadvantaged compared to others. The envious are afraid of losing something if they acknowledge that someone else has more. Therefore, they react with fear and hatred when confronted with someone else's good fortune, success or gifts, and try automatically to deprive the other of his or her happiness. Their eyes are sealed because the envious could not endure seeing the envied object or the joy of others and because the envious cannot see and value objectively. The penalties in Purgatory heal the wounds of the sin, which again is redeemed through confrontation. The envious now really cannot see what they could not "see" because of envy.

At the same time, having their eyes stitched together remedies the root cause of envy: the fear. Dante refers to the habit in his time of sewing together the eyes of "a haggard hawk".[3] This is comparable to the use of hoods in falconry. The purpose is to remove from view anything that the bird is afraid of, aggressive towards or nervous about, and to allow a gradual exposure to light and sight. Finally, the wire can be fully removed.

The envious experience this gradual undoing of envy while learning about generosity, the virtue corresponding to envy, in a similar way. Again, fear is the basis for envy, particularly fear of any form of giving – from allowing others their possessions to granting another success. It is therefore understandable that generosity is most feared by the envious. It seems to threaten their whole way of existence.

Because the envious cannot see, instead they hear disembodied voices speaking of the virtue of generosity. The voices evoke the delight of love: love of others, love for friends and love of enemies. "Blessed are the Merciful" is the benediction for the envious. Compassion, the direct opposite of envy, has the effect on the envious that it gradually opens their eyes to the value of generosity and sympathy. When the eyes are open they see the reflection of the angel of generosity and experience its multiplying effect. Their transformation lies in their realizing how fear and envy restrict the scope of view and growth in general: "The more aspirants to that bliss are multiplied, more good there is to love, and more is lov'd; as mirrors, that reflect, each unto other, propagated light."[4]

It is one thing to understand that reciprocity in love increases love, just as spiritual goods augment by sharing. But to understand how and why to love those who impart injury is to take generosity a step further: it is what eventually sets the envious free to move on to the next level.

Personal developmental aspects of envy and generosity

Psychologically speaking, envy[5] and generosity form two sides of the same coin: they depend on connection with others. Leaders who experience envy are frequently high-functioning, good performers. In addition they have a busy social schedule. They have in common a relational pattern of seeking others – either to own or to destroy.

There is also envy-based generosity, false generosity made up of a combination of envy and envy-informed generosity that tries to restrain others out of fear. We see this in the envious leader who feels as if their life depends on the goodwill of others. They fear this dependency, and when caught in envy, try to destroy the good in others. When caught in false generosity, on the other hand, there is no end to their giving, because they feel their life depends on it. Both envy and this form of false generosity are directed outward and impel an individual to outward action. In psychology, dependent narcissism is one term that applies to the condition of the envious.

Envy is indeed a very undesirable emotion and not readily available for scrutiny because most people do not want to acknowledge their envy, least of all talk about it. Envy is hidden. That is why much comprehensive analysis of envy refers to fictive characters from mythology, literature, film or other art forms.

The fairy tale of *Cinderella* is a well-known example of envy in action.[6] Cinderella's secret is that she had a mother who loved her and provided the spiritual connection that protected her. On her deathbed she had said, "Dear child, be good and pious, and then the good God will always protect you, and I will look down on you from Heaven and be near you." This connection to something larger than herself, beyond life, was the resource in Cinderella that enabled her to stay close to her own essence and not become caught in envy's destruction. It was also what fuelled the envy of the stepsisters. They, in contrast, were brought up to represent and to seek their value in material goods. They gave her increasingly daunting tasks such as sorting the lentils that the stepmother had thrown in the ashes. The fact that Cinderella's intrinsic value did not seem to give in to their attacks only increased their resentment, as these factors turned into a critique of their existence, and they could not bear even looking at her.

The perspective of the stepsisters shows us that an envious person will never see the position of the envied. The evil stepsisters will never consider that Cinderella is really doing her best in the midst of deprivation. The more good the envied one does, the more he or she gives, the worse it gets. Once the dynamics between envy and generosity have been constellated, they tend to accelerate. It is the inner poverty in the stepsisters and stepmother that fuels their envy; inner poverty, stemming from alienation from the Self, the inner core that is projected externally and perceived as unobtainable, hateful, and therefore has to be destroyed.

What role in this envy – generosity tale did Cinderella play? As for envy, we see how Cinderella needed to learn to recognize envy not only in the sisters and the stepmother, but through them also in herself. They brought to her attention her own unconscious envy of them. It is not difficult to imagine her being envious of the stepsisters, who have a mother who is still alive, a father (hers) who protects them (not her), and lavish opportunities while being groomed for the prince. Moving beyond the obvious form of envy as displayed by the sisters, let us turn to Cinderella's envy, which is hidden in complacency. What Cinderella may not have seen is that the stepsisters had to pay with their souls and that their mother treated them as objects in pursuit of her own imagined "career" at the castle. If Cinderella had been allowed to deny envy, to remain in the attitude of "I don't know why they are so mean to me," she would have remained naive. And in that frame of mind she would also remain the victim, the one who is always doing her best, but never gets any credit for it. Cinderella was – perhaps, thanks to the challenges from sisters and stepmother – almost forced to become aware of the polarities of good and bad, persona and shadow within herself. She could do this because she managed to accept her faith and the feelings that came with it – suffering, helplessness, poverty and isolation. Beyond something like taking life as it comes, this means trusting in the fundamental way that life takes care of you. It is interesting to note that it was her spiritual conviction that supported her maturation as an individual.

Turning to generosity, we see different aspects of it in Cinderella's response to envy. At first it was expressed in her giving in to the stepsisters' demands; she would just give and do more. This form of generosity, on the one hand, shows us there is no way around seemingly endless work if you want to get what you want (go to the ball), but on the other hand, it represents the form of false generosity that falls into the same logic as envy, that is, it restricts and works around negative emotions, in this case Cinderella's fear that things would get worse or that she would be further deprived of possibilities. False generosity is a form of manipulation. It differs from generosity as defined by Dante by its reductive objective. Dante's generosity recognizes the value of participation and open-handed yielding, its aim being to see the multiplying effect of good.

Leadership development through envy and generosity

Envy and generosity are part of most of our interactions at work. Any comparison among groups or individuals prompts that. Comparisons occur on so many levels, and although not always relevant for a particular job or project, they are a tacit basis for our relationships.

As established by William James, a psychologist of religion, envy is most significant if it falls in a person's area of identification.[7] When people see themselves as for instance a mediator, then when someone else is mediating a conflict more successfully and outperforms them, they feel more envious than when confronted with someone who is a wonderful gardener or chess player, which they have no aspiration for. In addition, envy tends to become constellated more often and more ferociously among people who are close in some kind of pecking order. Any kind of ranking can have a subjective basis; someone can feel ahead or above someone else without it being verified by any outer distinction. Envy or competition in such settings is different from objective rankings in an established hierarchy, which tend to lead to more political fights.

In the subjective setting, the envious person often feels that the envied enjoys benefits by sheer coincidence or luck. It can be that the envied won the lottery, got a position through fortunate circumstances – benefits that cannot really be acquired but which are still accorded a person without any logical reason. The envious feels that it is undeserved.

Gossip, a form of manipulation, is one of the most overt, active forms of envy. It is the envious way of discharging some of the feelings of inferiority and at the same time deprecating the value of the envied. Being successful may cause others to give you nicknames, typically targeting something negative and shifting the comparison away from what you are good at.

Probably one of the few paths a leader has at disposal is to set out to turn envy into positive good – to emulate what is evoked by envy. Being envious is a signal that what you long for is now ready to be explored and developed. What you long for is now close enough to be integrated. When you have made whatever quality that is 'yours' and truly own it, you can share it freely. Leadership is an exercise in creating real opportunities for people to become as good as they wish to be. And the art in that is neither to be tempted to bully people around nor to generously grant other people's every whim.

Let us now look at the path of regaining power and freedom to own such power that can lead to unbound generosity.

Dante shows us yet one more quality that is relevant today:

> By how much more they call it ours,
> So much propriety of each in good
> Increases more, and heighten'd charity
> Wraps that fair cloister in a brighter flame.[8]

The voices of generosity in Purgatory speak of friendship and understanding whose essence is sharing. It can mean, for instance, the consciousness of a portion of shared destiny – what happens to one person, let us say a shareholder, to some degree also happens to the peers. Likewise, kindness that is loving responds to the needs of the people you work with. It tends to augment and set the tone for much interaction beyond the actual moment of exchange. The realization that sharing also means receiving, that allowing someone to make an effort for you, to accept, and to acknowledge that openly, is another form of generosity based on sharing.

Sharing generosity differs from the kind of generosity that is a manipulative way of controlling others and is exhausting for the person who gives. The major difference for leadership is that rather than having a restraining effect it boosts creativity. A living work ethic, taking the notion of equal sharing into consideration in the cultivation of generosity rather than envy, must allow room for appreciation of another, whether deserving it or not. It requires continuous stimulation of your colleagues to sense the freedom to be totally happy for another person, whether they are successful in competing areas, in other areas, or not at all. This can lead to a new level of friendship that transcends notions such as liking, not liking, or agreement and disagreement. It leads to inclusion based on equality.

Reflections on generosity

Renée Frissen

When I started OpenEmbassy in 2015, many people from Syria and Eritrea were applying for asylum in the Netherlands due to the political situation in their countries. My first son had just been born and I was home on maternity leave with little interaction in the external world. However, there was so much news covering this immigration, that I followed and soon felt involved in the situation.

I encountered a woman who worked for an emergency shelter, and even at this time there was already a large community of Amsterdam residents who wanted to contribute to the lives of their new neighbors. She was excellent in creating engagement, but there remained room for improvement on the practical side of things. My management experience meant I could really help with the organization. I volunteered to work behind the scenes and create schedules, logistics, contact information – simple but essential structures. The work fitted perfectly with my schedule, first at home with my son, later alongside my full-time work.

Community engagement

When I discussed this with others, I realized people were very willing to contribute, although mostly online. I sensed an opportunity. My research on modern voluntary work revealed that the Netherlands has the largest rate of volunteerism in Europe. However, the existing pool is ageing, and the younger group I spoke with didn't feel called to step into the current formula, which entails much fieldwork and little flexibility. That was my first observation.

Second, many newcomers received temporary residency and were relocated to different Dutch cities and villages. Then they experienced two things: loneliness and complexity. The buzz and interactivity in

Amsterdam was replaced by silence and they had to deal with so many new things and situations. They were more or less lost in the system.

So my inquiry continued: "what if we could connect those who are prepared to work online with those who need help?" That's how OpenEmbassy was born. Together with Ahmad, a Syrian software developer, I set up a helpdesk early in 2016. Today we have seven employees on the payroll, four freelancers and a community of 8,000 members, distributed over more than half of all the municipalities in the Netherlands.

Change from within

After one year, I analyzed the questions reaching the helpdesk and found two categories. One, the pure practicalities pertaining to being "new", not Dutch. And two, the structural issues inherent to dysfunctional bureaucratic systems that hindered newcomers' ability to build their lives according to their ambitions. As I thought about the second category, I began to realize that by simply assisting in solving these issues, we would be upholding the flaws, not eliminating them.

So, I remodeled the concept and changed the organization so that it helps identify and improve the system from within. Although the helpdesk is still at the core of our operation, today the system is our client. The newcomers remain the target of our support, but we serve them better by assisting multiple public organizations and sectors to adjust and improve outdated policies.

The people who need us are central

We take the voice, and thus the experience and knowledge, of the newcomers as our starting point.

Through a carefully designed set of questions and methodology, we learn a great deal about our own bureaucratic system. The method is primarily interactive. We select issues that we believe can be improved and work on them with representatives from the different public organs providing aid. We aim for pragmatic solutions that provide incremental benefits, for newcomers as well as the employees of these organizations.

This focus on the newcomers is very radical. It might seem strange, but the bureaucratic systems simply never ask them what they know or need. At the core, we are about building communities, online as well as offline. Community is the most ancient form of organization, and the most modern one. All tech development is based on community building.

How we work

We have two groups of employees – action researchers and community managers. The knowledge we build is around how to live together in settings of difference and diversity. This is highly topical at the moment, and applicable for a great variety of communities – companies, healthcare, education, you name it.

I regularly assess whether our impact matches our talents and skills. We assist many individuals in finding language buddies, internships and jobs. We support talented newcomers in building a network and reaching their ambition, as well as vulnerable people, like young single mothers and the homeless. But we also help change policy, teach civil servants how to put inclusion into practice, and inspire employers to hire newcomers.

The office is very diverse. One-third have a refugee background, including a woman who has been in the Netherlands for a long time and knows firsthand about the integration process and about building a life here.

A modern meeting culture

Our regular Monday team meetings are limited to about 30 minutes, but we manage to share the goals for the week – "What do you need from whom to realize your goal?" In this way, we are all involved and share successes as well as learning points. Informal feedback is important and together we stimulate that culture.

In addition, I conduct weekly half hour, one-on-one meetings. It creates space to lead and mentor, and provides an opportunity for individual employees to have my full attention for whatever they want to talk about, beyond their targets. And every six months we have development offsites to jointly determine the goals for the company and individual colleagues. There must be a match between the role and the personality.

How I lead

For me as a leader, it is both a strategic trajectory and an organic process. My career will always be geared towards social problem solving, with an entrepreneurial spirit. Why? The problems that arise when people live together are very complex and have a great impact on society. Tackling the issues – the human factor – requires multiple skillsets, coordination and positive energy. It's a tough assignment, and that is exactly why

I like it. Moreover, injustice really affects me on all levels: physical, emotional, moral. I become beset with such an urge to at least *try* to contribute to respectful solutions. That's why.

Managing our larger team (the community) from a distance is different to managing the immediate team. People stay in our community because they can contribute, learn and receive. Our job is not so much to manage them, as to nurture this exchange.

It might sound odd, but as a leader I have learned from negative examples from academia to entrepreneurs, where leaders have failed to take care of their people. Just being allowed to excel in a purpose-driven organization doesn't mean that all other needs are met. People need to feel involved, seen, heard and appreciated. And I see it as an important part of my job to ensure that occurs.

The global visions that drive me

I manage in accordance with my two key global visions: radical equality and community. Generosity is only valuable if there is true equality. You may donate time, know-how, etc., but if the underlying perspective is pity and inequality, it is one-sided generosity – not an equal relationship. This can even be harmful. "The road to Hell is paved with good intentions" applies here and to the whole antiquated system.

Our job is to release the potential for true generosity – person to person – which rewards in respectful ways. Everyone benefits. Learning by doing, seeing, hearing and most of all: listening. Openhandedness is perhaps the key factor here. To sincerely acknowledge the other in the role they play, whatever their role, age, race, gender, religion and experience.

Notes

1 René Girard defined the notion of mimetic desire – the desire to mirror and match what others are doing – and it is not directed towards a desired object, a commodity. He describes mimetic desire as a cause of conflict, but also as the driving force of our culture. See, for example, Girard (2004).
2 See, for example, Klein (1988), Stein (1996).
3 Alighieri, D. *The Divine Comedy II: Purgatory*, Canto XIII: 70. Translation by the Rev. H.F. Cary, M.A. Urbana, IL: Project Gutenberg. Retrieved 5 June 2019 from www.gutenberg.org/ebooks/8795.
4 Alighieri, D. *The Divine Comedy II: Purgatory*, Canto XV: 73–75. Translation by the Rev. H.F. Cary, M.A. Urbana, IL: Project Gutenberg. Retrieved 5 June 2019 from www.gutenberg.org/ebooks/8795.
5 The study of envy in psychology has been largely influenced by the work of Melanie Klein (1988). In her book on envy and gratitude, Melanie Klein

defines envy as hostility towards what is perceived as good. Envy, she says, is an attack on life itself in the form of an external object (the mother's breast) on which the ego is utterly dependent. She believed that this form of very early primary envy is the process underlying other forms of envy.

6 For a comprehensive analysis, see Ulanov and Ulanov (2008).
7 James, W. (1890). *The Principles of Psychology*. Boston, MA: Henry Holt.
8 Alighieri, D. *The Divine Comedy II: Purgatory*, Canto XV: 54–57. Translation by the Rev. H.F. Cary, M.A. Urbana, IL: Project Gutenberg. Retrieved 5 June 2019 from www.gutenberg.org/ebooks/8795.

Chapter 5

Anger and gentleness

We encounter anger, or wrath (the Dantean term), in many forms on a daily basis. Hot or cold, direct or meandering, a simmering or sudden outburst – we know them all. Contrary to envy, openly displayed and self-reported anger is abundant and readily available for public scrutiny. Apart from physical pain and threats, among the most common reasons for anger are insult, betrayal, someone else failing or being incompetent, and, of course, being the target of someone else's aggression. Feeling hurt arouses a desire to take revenge on the cause of that hurt. We become angry because of something, and target the reason, or what seems to be the reason, or what is convenient, such as a scapegoat. We often experience anger as a blend of pain and pleasure – the pain of being hurt and the pleasure from revenge and acting out the anger. Therefore, in anger there is both pleasure and power. That is why anger so easily gets out of hand.

The more we are aware of the dynamics of anger, the more we notice that some of the behaviors of others that trigger our anger are behaviors we would gladly engage in ourselves. This is a double standard, often linked to power structures, such as employer-employee, mother-daughter, father-son. Without being aware of your own anger, the opposites of power and powerlessness are easily acted out between a boss and an employee. Whose emotion is it? Without knowing, the vicious circle of revenge is set in motion. For leaders who operate competitively, it is almost mandatory to know the flavors of anger and to find out how to deal with this sometimes overwhelming rush.

Gentleness is the virtue that counters anger. It is patient and peaceful – by comparison, a state very different from anger. At first glance, it is difficult to imagine how anger and gentleness are interrelated because their outward expressions are truly opposite. Examining them more closely though, we can see that the underlying theme that links them both is "acceptance". Gentleness takes its strength from being firmly rooted and flexible. It is like the allusion to a willow tree that is often used in martial arts training to foster the right feeling in the adept. A judoka must be flexible, resilient and rooted. Stiff resistance or heated aggression will not suffice to endure the tests and attacks of the game. For this purpose, self-discipline is an important part of such training.

Gentleness, like anger, accepts a provocation, but rather than responding with vengeance, gentleness evokes a response of forbearance. It is as if when anger prompts an individual to immediate retaliation, gentleness waits for a moment to forgive and forget. Both anger and gentleness are equally injured and powerless, and they have the same level of endurance, but they bring about very different actions.

The difficulty, though, for many leaders I have worked with is to strike the right balance between aggression and gentleness. They feel that they easily fall into a box of being seen as either aggressors or wimps. This may well reflect stereotypes of colleagues, but can also mirror low awareness or an undifferentiated relationship to anger and gentleness. In any case, by examining these poles you can learn how to respond to and express anger and gentleness more consciously and with greater variety. The next generation of leaders has the opportunity to do just that.

Anger and gentleness in Dante's Purgatory

As Dante and Virgil approach the third level, where anger is purged, they are immersed in black smoke. From having suffered with the blind in the level of envy, then having seen the sun again and felt the relief of gratitude for the light, they are once more in the dark. The cloud of black smoke that surrounds the angry ones is an image of the state the angry are in: blinded by rage, they cannot see clearly. The angry thus cannot see, but they can hear; they move forward by careful listening. Confrontation with the sin of anger, which is its remedy, is a struggle to accept circumstances and win by means of what is available: "and since the cloudy smoke, Forbids the seeing, hearing in its stead, Shall keep us join'd".[1]

Dante says about anger (*ira*) that it is "excessive love of justice perverted to revenge and spite". It is too much a conviction of being right but not recognized for that, and so is accompanied by the feeling you are being unfairly treated. Dante himself admits to anger in the sense of his excessive sense of righteousness. It is not difficult to see how anger is linked to pride, another sin Dante admitted to. Significant for anger, which likens it to pride, is its most imminent danger – it divides and separates:

I journey'd through that bitter air and foul,
Still list'ning to my escort's warning voice,
'Look that from me thou part not.'[2]

Virgil's warning is twofold: anger creates division between people, and it also separates you from your own good judgment and reason, from your senses. Anger distorts perception so judgment becomes clouded. With a very narrow scope of perception, we do not know what we are doing, yet feel overwhelmed by the urge for revenge to do anything. Consequently, the exercise for the wrathful is to pray together in perfect unison, thereby learning how to unite in harmony. They sing the litany of the Lamb of God, *Agnus Dei*, which through its mercy takes away the stains of anger and gives peace. The next attainment on the level of anger is to endure and patiently work towards peace.

Dante meets Marco Lombardo, a Venetian known for his hot temper, and explores with him the relationship between anger, which is destructive, and righteous indignation, which can be constructive. But when is anger justified and when is it sinful? Dante's anger and charge were directed towards the Church, which he felt had given up its spirituality in exchange for wealth and power. The question at hand was whether the Church was corrupt because of Heaven, determinism, or for earthly reasons, as a result of free will. Lombardo answered that humanity has just as much responsibility as God for the well-being of creation: "If then in the present race of mankind err, Seek in yourselves the cause, and find it there."[3] Their conversation shows that personal responsibility and political integrity are essential precisely when circumstances do not favor them. If everything were to be the result of determinism, then whatever a person does, cannot be rewarded or punished. And if there is no reason to be angry about it, anger becomes useless and loses its compelling force. You can have it or not have it, it does not matter.

If, on the other hand, you accept free will, you have a choice how to respond, whether anger is justified or not. Exercising mildness or peacefulness of mind in the face of hurtful hindrances and perceived injustice brings the angry person to a realization of causality, and that to some extent we cannot know what the meaning of right or wrong is in the bigger picture. Love is the root of all action, good or bad. A forgiving approach to friends and foes might be just as motivated as a vindictive one.

Leaving lower Purgatory, Virgil reviews the work accomplished thus far and puts it in context. The first three sins are caused by love perverted. We now see what that means in practice: it means that you cannot appreciate and enjoy God's creation with submission, gratitude and peacefulness. The virtue of gentleness on the other hand is more interesting, more powerful because it is redeeming.

But let us first look closely at anger, or rage, imagining its feeling state, its drive and its consequences.

Personal developmental aspects of anger and gentleness

The desire for revenge, whether it arises from insult or betrayal, is embedded in distrust and a sense of having been unjustly or unfairly treated. It's a familiar theme: if a person hurts you, especially someone you thought you could trust and rely on, your anger causes you to want to retaliate and hurt back, just as you have been hurt. If we allow this desire for revenge to go uninterrupted and unmitigated, the target becomes clear, the focus single-minded, with no space for reconsideration, shame or perspective. Anger is very persuasive, and all too easily we readily embrace anger, especially anger that we consider justified or morally required. In the face of injustice or violence, we are expected to be outraged. Often, our anger has pushed us past the point of being capable of discussion, reflection or any other kind of interaction with the person who we consider has wronged us. Numerous examples exist in pop culture, including movies and television shows, of characters who are so consumed with anger and their desire for retaliation that it not only undermines but destroys their capacity for love, including self-love. They portray – in at times extreme situations – the interplay between the fundamental aspects of anger: betrayal, revenge and justification. Something happens that is perceived as a transgression, and the character self-righteously desires vengeance for it. It follows a pattern of conflict, aggression, justification, proving the emotional value to being right by setting things straight, and the blind inability to see the perspective of the other. They also show us their vulnerability, hurt, distrust, fear, and, finally, the shame that follows aggression. We see how anger can pull a person together and how it can lead to utter fragmentation. It shows the two-facedness of anger, with its possibly devastating consequences and its life-giving force, a force that can mobilize a person to escape from an undesirable life setting. In that sense anger constitutes an ethical dilemma.

There are countries where a public display of uncontrolled anger, especially acted out in large groups, is viewed positively – particularly forms of romantic anger. The anger of contemporary Dutch corporate life is not of this order. So, although a typical leadership profile shows traits that match all the revenge ingredients discussed above, that is, planning, goal setting, endurance, focus, will, resilience and the ability to cope with the unexpected, we do not typically witness it at work. In ordinary everyday life, we do not see this so clearly displayed as in the film. There are good reasons for that, reasons we can all imagine that relate to what one can lose in becoming a roaming rampage of revenge. Although anticipation of consequences often prevents outbursts of anger, this does not deny the fact that at some point in our lives almost all of us experience the feeling that urges us to retaliation. Nevertheless, the response is highly individual.

General displayed aggression leads to more forceful acting out. Repressed internalized anger, on the other hand, brings about more self-righteousness. We also know that overly controlled anger is one of the reasons for many forms of depression, illness and difficult relationships. Anger is a strong emotion that feels both bad and good.

Anger is often unavailable to us when perceived as uncomfortable. Fear is a reaction to anger that can disturb an immediate, spontaneous response to aggression. Fear of anger and of angry people is what prompts families, companies and whole societies to harbor and hide compulsively aggressive people. Without such fear, a raped woman would tell everyone who had raped her. A bullied child would cry for help. Fear is at the same time the most common reason for anger. We get angry in order to avoid feeling the hurt that holds the acknowledgment of our own vulnerability. As a consequence, we move further and further away from a direct experience of anger. We become afraid of acknowledging awareness of our anger.

Successful leaders in the Netherlands are skillful in controlling anger. Prevalent forms of controlled anger and leadership from a psychological perspective are obsessive compulsion and passive aggression. These are both ways of hiding anger. Anger and control go hand in hand because these two are extremes on the same emotional axes. Control has the function of putting a cap on an emotion because it is experienced as uncontrollable and consuming. Such basic conflict between rage and fear, which makes a person highly prone to anxiety, can be observed in obsessive compulsive disorders. People who were raised without warmth and forgiveness for faults, or were exposed to much injustice, premature responsibilities and overbearing control, can develop in this direction. In fact, obsessive compulsive disorders have been found to be the most common diagnosis in the West, and they are a frequently recognized trait among senior leaders. This form of anger can foster leaders who excel in efficiency, fault-tolerant systems and efficient follow-through. Obsessive compulsion is not flexible.

Passive aggression is a familiar yet tricky form of controlled anger. The strategy behind it aims at a sneaky comeuppance against someone viewed as powerful. It covertly obstructs their goals while hiding behind martyrdom. We see it in people who habitually provoke. It is in a person who persistently procrastinates, forgets or resorts to, "Sorry, but I tried my best," in response to failing to deliver. In their discontent they blame others for what is their fault and they refuse to acknowledge it. They will not rest until they "get you", until you have acted out their aggression. For the passive-aggressive person, the fault is with the world, and they are just poor victims of the unfair treatment of overpowering, impossible demands. The problem is that the passive-aggressive person is proficient in creating double binds, so once you are caught, it is very difficult to escape the dependency and stickiness of the conflict. It repeats and repeats, but never gets anywhere near resolution.

Controlled forms of anger and passive aggression are what we generally see in business. It can be recognized as frustration, reproach, resentment and manipulation. How can we work with it and develop its potentials? What hinders gentleness from being a more prevailing response?

Leadership development through anger and gentleness

In business, anger is often considered a way of taking a stand and setting things straight. In fact, there is often a feeling that too little anger is displayed, and people have been accused of not being angry enough, for not standing up for their rights. Many leaders are seen as weak if they are not angry enough.

In some views, however, no anger is never justified; there is no legitimate moral purpose that merits anger. From this perspective, anger is seen as degrading humanity and as dysfunctional; it cannot achieve anything that could not be better achieved in other ways. One underlying reason is that no single individual can have a full overview of all factors at play, and hence, the individual cannot truly estimate the justification for anger, which makes the whole logic of justified anger impossible.

Whatever leadership role you are in, you will be operating in a context that for decades has developed and refined methods of aggression. There is no way for you to withdraw from the objective reality of your environment and the fact that you are part of it; you are also capable of aggression. At the same time, in our culture and business environment, gentleness is frequently seen as a weakness and impossible for career purposes. But it is precisely in this setting, where anger and power are intimately linked, that gentleness and the ability to acknowledge being hurt or feeling weak will prove superior leadership.

Gentleness shows up "unseen and unbesought",[4] as is fitting to its nature.

Dante teaches us that anger places us in a cloud. As the Angel of Peace erases the third "P" on Dante's forehead, he feels as if he were brushed by the angel's wing, like a fresh breeze. A relief indeed, a breath of fresh air. He was filled with an unforgettable yearning, an endless, boundless longing for more

Gentleness of heart has such attraction. Once tasted, you will forever long for more.

Reflections on gentleness

Steven Knox[5]

A sense of proximity

Our hospital is one of the top clinical hospitals in the Netherlands. It's received the national annual award for best hospital multiple times.

When I was asked to take on my current role back in 2015, I gladly accepted for a number of reasons. One was that the hospital was quite advanced in terms of implementing technology to support effective healthcare. As an accountant with a PhD in information management, I saw opportunities to create healthcare that was modern, accessible to all, as well as being sustainable, as it would cater to my children's generation, who were born in an online world and take it for granted.

Second, the geographical accessibility is great in this region. Patients reach the hospital easily and find their way within the system effortlessly. It's important for a sense of safety, which I believe plays a big role in cure. We employ over 4,000 healthcare professionals and together they form the "spirit" of the hospital. In the time that I've been here, I've invested in creating a sense of proximity, a feeling on the wards of truly caring for each other as colleagues, with love and attention. Patients pick that up immediately and feel included. That's how it works.

Finally, the culture and communication of the hospital I worked at previously as Vice President did not go well with my personality. I experienced distance between people that did not make sense to me. For example, on the day of my mother's funeral, a close colleague called me. No condolences, no "how are you?", no support. Instead, they asked if I'd be attending a board meeting that same afternoon. I thought that odd, especially for a senior healthcare practitioner. This is but an illustration of a prevailing mindset with which I didn't feel at home. So, yes, in a sense I made a choice to move away from an unwanted environment, but most of all towards a future more conducive to modern healthcare.

The role of preventative healthcare

There are structural problems embedded in the healthcare system, which is only natural. The system was established for purposes that are no longer relevant today, and systems take time to shift. I believe in working from the periphery and offering innovative solutions. So, I'm committed to pursuing a mission for healthcare that is ready to meet the challenges we face now and in the near future.

In the past healthcare was about curing, and it still is, of course. You are ill; you want to be cured. But now, preventative healthcare is becoming increasingly important. As demographics show increasing lifespans, quality of life becomes central, and this perspective cascades into the lifestyle of younger generations who may wish to grow old with dignity.

Preventive healthcare can benefit enormously from AI and ways of monitoring and regulating body functions such as heart rate, activity, restfulness and sleep. It's nothing new: yogis are well aware of it, but the tools available today can assist large populations who are not trained yogis.

A vision of the future

The future of healthcare is holistic. Not simply because we now have the instruments to measure multiple functions simultaneously and correlate, compare, and so on. But more fundamentally because the mentality has changed. The body is not a thing out there, the mind not a separate entity in another place. It's an integrated whole. People get that. I believe that the fact that today 75 per cent of all doctors are women, and that women doctors tend to take a holistic view, is both a cause and a consequence of an overall changing mentality, conscious or not.

Today's hospitals won't be needed in the future. Today, 40 per cent of revenue is generated from chronically ill patients who will be treated elsewhere or hopefully not be needing healthcare. My ambition is to prepare this organization for that development. And that does not mean simply introducing a new app. Instead, it hinges on changing behaviors, shifting mindsets. It takes time and sensitivity, true listening.

Sensitivity and responsibility

I have come to believe that everyone is a leader. By "leader" I mean that each individual leads their own life and as such interacts with others from that perspective. And only from that starting point is it possible to make a positive difference. Childhood experiences are formative for the way we lead our lives. My early years certainly made me into who I am and determine to a large extent how I lead my life and even this organization.

I was the third child in the family. My mother had wanted a girl and was quite open about that, so, I was treated like a girl. Learned about colors, cooking, kindness to others . . . things considered more "feminine", at least at the time. My father, on the other hand, was a very angry and abusive man. I turned out to become a highly sensitive person with problems trusting in others – my trust must be earned. Real affection I've learned from my children.

I need time on my own when I want to feel in touch with my emotions. For instance, I might drive my car for long distances for a day or two, just listening to music, no distraction such as the cellphone. Just me, alone with myself. Slowly this experience inevitably leads into a very powerful sense of wholeness, which later helps me re-enter the world of other people and their needs and expectations in a state of calm. I see it as a discipline and as a responsibility, for myself mainly, for leading my life consciously.

The personal is integral to the professional

My personal development translates into my professional work, particularly when creating a culture of health, and healthy relationships. I have just implemented a decision I took long ago, to forbid smoking on the premises of the hospital. No special smoking areas; no smoking, full stop. It's no news that smoking is detrimental to health. But, what I've witnessed here in terms of smoking-related suffering is just beyond words. It took time to implement the ban, because it's a sensitive issue, but finally I decided, this cannot go on, not here. And it's working.

I also want to stimulate physical activities across the hospital. One of our top diabetes specialists showed me his research, revealing that if each of his patients took one 30-minute walk each week, there would be significant health improvements.

I decided to set an example, and so I regularly bike, swim in the river and work out at the gym together with different colleagues. It's so rewarding, all that positive energy. I see the colleagues who join me, including those who organize publicity for the sports-related fundraising we contribute to, as ambassadors for the healthy physical activity I want this hospital to stand for.

Third, and this is still in incubation, is nutrition. I want to make people more aware that what you eat and drink matters for your health.

Sugar is not just found in old-school soft drinks and candy; it's also in the latest products. And it's very much present in alcohol. To this day, our receptions and celebrations are filled to the brim with wine and fatty snacks. It's perceived as generous and festive, and I get this – but is it really the best idea? This is a longer-term issue, but it's important to me to see that it can be changed. Habits can be broken.

Genuine connection

Healthy relationships start with communication: how we interact. Is there a tone of tact, decency, collegial appreciation, respect and gentility? How are you with the other? How do you enter a conflict? How do you hold your ground gracefully? This is what counts today.

Much internal communication occurs online, including via Facebook. And it may sometimes serve as a covert way of bullying. That's why we have a 24/7-communication department watching over social media. I get a text message immediately when abuse is reported. Sometimes I wake up due when I receive one at night, and having a hard time getting back to sleep, pondering, "Is this really a serious professional, at my hospital, who wrote this? I hadn't expected that." It's too easy to damage others, just because of a lack of proximity, and this hurts me. I deal with these situations by speaking directly to the reported person early the next morning. I ask what seems to be the problem and query if there's a better way of handling it. My nonverbal communication makes it quite clear that this communication had been hurtful.

This re-establishes a connection and means we can talk and resolve the conflict. Because genuine connection fosters a form of gentleness that's indispensable for success.

Notes

1 Alighieri, D. (2004). *The Divine Comedy II: Purgatory*, Canto XVI: 35–36. Translation by the Rev. H.F. Cary, M.A. Urbana, IL: Project Gutenberg. Retrieved 5 June 2019 from www.gutenberg.org/ebooks/8795.
2 Alighieri, D. (2004). *The Divine Comedy II: Purgatory*, Canto XVI: 13–15. Translation by the Rev. H.F. Cary, M.A. Urbana, IL: Project Gutenberg. Retrieved 5 June 2019 from www.gutenberg.org/ebooks/8795.
3 Alighieri, D. (2004). *The Divine Comedy II: Purgatory*, Canto XVI: 82–83. Translation by the Rev. H.F. Cary, M.A. Urbana, IL: Project Gutenberg. Retrieved 5 June 2019 from www.gutenberg.org/ebooks/8795.
4 Alighieri, D. (1955). *The Divine Comedy II: Purgatory*, Canto XVI: 47, commentary. Translation by Dorothy L. Sayers. London: Penguin Classics.
5 This is a pseudonym.

Chapter 6

Sloth and zeal

A sloth is an animal that lives in the trees and cannot walk on the ground, but drags itself around. It is supposed to be the slowest mammal on Earth. Sloth as a sin is sluggish laziness, and it does not seem to go together with leadership. We imagine leaders as energetic, hardworking and with foresight, continuously creating more and more value. In fact, what leader would demonstrate anything other than zeal, eager dedication and intense enthusiasm?

Sloth however presents a problem in society, and in the end its leaders are held responsible. Take the example of general elections. In the Netherlands, compulsory voting was rescinded in 1970, resulting in substantially lower turnouts. Young people and first-time voters in particular do not care to vote. Inquiry into the reasons why they did not participate showed that many felt they were too busy and did not have time to vote. But according to subsequent research, there was no objective decrease in leisure time that can substantiate this explanation. This would be an example of sloth in the form of insufficient commitment and determination. There are other voices claiming that increasing disinterest in voting is caused by the complacency of politicians who only seem to care about winning, not about the engagement of the voters; they show alienation and a mindset of "who cares, we won". Research shows that generation Z feels overlooked and powerless by the political system, which in their view is in for an overhaul. Party politics is a thing of the past.[1] In this case sloth would be the politicians' lack of interest in creating trust and clarity about their policies and invest in renewal.

We can also recognize this pattern in companies and corporate boards. It is the duty of the board and its chairman to ensure that the values, integrity and purpose of an organization are honored with respect to all stakeholders. Yet, we see examples of sloth in the lack of control or critique of leaders that allows them to develop a mentality harmful to their companies and employees. Sloth can then turn into a more widespread company culture. Some people lose the desire to perform in a context of laziness. They do not feel the need or the room to set themselves apart so instead they just coast along.

We see sloth in the absence of interest that runs through self-selected monocultures of lemmings, those who neglect problems and fail to pursue their duties. It is a collusion to refuse to know or to pursue the truth. Such groupthink is composed of individuals who exhibit a psychic retreat from what they know is right and pertinent. Groupthink is contagious and an aspect of sloth. Tolerance is a strong principle in Dutch society that does not always reflect this lack of interest but it can do so. Disinterest can reflect such tolerance, which might turn into willingness to consider anything without any inner knowledge – anything goes.

Sloth sometimes imitates zeal. It mimics the ways of a person who is passionately devoted and working with determination for a noble cause. In fact, in highly developed economies, frantic activity is perhaps the most common form of sloth. It does not take into account the benefit of reflection. At work we say there is no time for reflection, and conclude that all energy goes into handling the daily operational stuff, stuff that will never be ready. That is when we lose our overview and in the end our sense of purpose. Instead, we give in to overcharged mental and physical activities, being busy, so busy that we do not have time to take in exactly what we are busy with, or why, or for what purpose.

This has led to counter movements, so-called sloth clubs, with slogans such as "Slow is beautiful." Their aim is to counter the despondency of societies that continually run around, and instead create a harmonious alternative that is low in energy consumption, ecological, and allows a slow pace in business and life in general – in other words, sustainable. The name should not mislead us to underestimate the amount of work involved in preparing slow food, but rather to point at the purposeful engagement, love and attention to the activity of cooking that it denotes.

Sloth and zeal in Dante's Purgatory

Dante encounters sloth (*accidia*) on the fourth level. It is the sin in the middle, the one that divides the lower sins from the three upper ones. Unlike the others, sloth is not about too much or too little love. It is the sin of no love at all, a permanent state of indifference. It is failure to pursue the love of God with one's whole will. In Dorothy L. Sayers' words: "It is not mere idleness of mind and laziness of body: it is that whole poisoning of the will which, beginning with indifference and an attitude of 'I could not care less,' extends to the deliberate refusal of joy and culminates in morbid introspection and despair."[2] Sloth is redeemed by work alone; labor is the prayer of the slothful.

Because of its position, it has been suggested that sloth permeates both the preceding and the following levels. It can perhaps be likened to the solar plexus of the body associated with our will. When the solar plexus is deficient, it will not let energy through from the lower body, which represents functions such as grounding and drive, to the upper centers of feeling, thinking and spiritual awareness. And the upper part of the body will not connect with the lower, so there is a separation and no alignment, and no real direction in life because the will is stuck. In this sense, it is possible to understand the position of sloth and zeal as one of regulation and coordination, impacting all else. This is different from pride, which is the root cause: self-love that seeks to stand above everyone, cutting a person off from all of creation.

Sloth is about love that is absent, rendering a person insufficiently purposeful and weak, thrown by an invisible force between escapism and hopelessness. With senses numbed, with no direction coming from the senses to select and direct the attention, and with no passion for a real other person, it is as if life itself is no longer present. It is as if the spirit is gone but the person is kept alive.

It is night when Dante and Virgil arrive at sloth, and according to the rules in Purgatory they cannot move on but must sit down. Dante asks Virgil about love and free will, and asks Virgil to define the love that reduces all virtuous actions and their contrary sins. Virgil's reply has bearing on fundamental leadership concerns. He says that love itself is all good, but that loving all is not. It is the form of love that matters. When our senses are attracted to and choose an object to which love subsequently yields, there is a proper relationship between love and the object of love. Translated into a leadership context, that means that for every decision the leader needs to consult an inner compass and look at what it is drawn to and why, if this is the right direction or a pursuit that is appropriate at that time. Taking a decision just for the sake of it, or just because you can, or without conferring with others, may quickly damage a company's intrinsic values.

Then Virgil adds one thing. He says that this – to choose and give in to the choice – is as far as we can understand love, the rest must be left to Beatrice. Viewed from a leadership perspective, this could mean that you should pay attention to your decision-making and go for it, but then you have to let go. Do not make the mistake of thinking you have the power to correctly assess all aspects of the universe in which your action occurs. You are governed by forces beyond your control and scope of comprehension, and that is a fact worth acknowledging. Whatever your definition of that other "bigger-than-you" is, recognizing the notion of such existence paradoxically helps you to do your best in the face of challenging choices. It is as if it helps you to dare express your best judgment. It is as if you were supported by that contact to take seriously your share of what needs to be done. Otherwise, you could simply just pursue subjectively motivated impulses with no second thoughts or consideration of outcomes, blaming circumstances for any possible negative consequence.

As Virgil closes his argument, Dante, typically eager to learn more, allows his mind to wander, and he dozes off. Such is the contagious effect of sloth. Dante has a dream. He dreams of the Siren and her song. It is the most poignant dream of *The Divine Comedy* and reminds us of the revelation-like effect that dreams can have on our consciousness. It helps us see things and once we have done so, we can never again fall into oblivion. When we discuss leadership development later in this chapter, we will take a closer look at this dream and its message about the choices we make, whether consciously or not, about our identity.

Personal developmental aspects of sloth and zeal

Psychologically sloth is manifested in two major forms: first, in the form of laziness that diminishes any type of activity, physical, emotional, mental or spiritual; second, in the form of over-activity that propels a person to random, frantic running around or being all over the place. This is an inversion of the first form of sloth. It masks unwillingness or inability to endure the hard work of focusing on what really needs attention and what matters for development.

Zeal, the virtue that balances sloth, comes into action through work, "to labor is to pray".[3] The kind of work that zeal represents has a specific meaning. It does not necessarily mean action or doing things in themselves. Instead, zeal is about freely following the direction pointed out by the thing that matters at the moment. In analytical psychology the term libido stands for the energy that connects a person to life. C.G. Jung describes it as "a desire or impulse which is unchecked by any kind of authority, moral or otherwise. Libido is appetite in its natural state".[4] From the perspective of the psyche as a reality that cannot be exhaustively managed by rational and devised goals, it follows that libido, the life force, is endowed with intentionality. It "knows" the best direction for the overall well-being of a person before that has become fully conscious. Jung likens libido to water, and says that it must have a gradient if it is to flow. Dreams can reveal some of the inclination and direction of libido and show us how it operates. Libido is potential power for transformation, and it is sometimes hard work to follow it, just as it is hard work to resist and suppress it.

In Dante's language the term "passion" as an expression of zeal would come close to libido. In one embodiment of zeal, Dante speaks of Mary, who *ran* to tell her friend Elizabeth about the visit of the Archangel Gabriel and the annunciation. Mary did not sit and mull over the message, she did not question it, or repress enthusiasm or forecast difficulties. No, she had an immediate response, and she followed the energy with action, living it with the full involvement of her whole being. This is what zeal means: that we dare to live all the way, not knowing what is coming next, trusting that our life force "knows" where it is taking us, and that that is good.

It is an understatement to say that not all people experience this at all times. In fact, it is probably more likely that all people encounter the conflict of this central sin and virtue on a regular basis. There are times when the life force does not freely flow into will and determination. But this is not necessarily a problem. Through my research on spiritual development in the context of Sufi teachings,[5] I have come to realize that all potential development and transformation necessarily entails phases of doubt, of no hope, and no energy to care about what happens or to move on. Without such a stage of disillusionment, spiritual sloth, no new layer of spiritual awareness can emerge, and no new insights and illusions will become available to embrace.

Although common to spiritual seekers and people in general, it does make a difference how such passing sloth is received by the individual. It can be received with willingness to let it come and to let it go away again; somehow, paradoxically to allow it to "flow" – just as the life force does. But then again it can be received with rejection by a person who only wants the good life force flow. This approach can easily lead to bitterness and disappointment. I have seen it in hard-working senior managers and in advanced spiritual teachers who feel, and rightly so, that they have devoted all their lives to their career or spiritual practice and now, instead of reward for their investment, they get this, a barrier in the road. They feel that their hard work merits a promotion. But it is a mistake, because generally true promotions cannot be earned. They just happen. After unceasing hard work, there is now doubt through a complex set of circumstances and conditions, including the gradient of your own essence. But if a person does not allow it to happen, that person will become blocked. The block can be in the form of outer obstacles, as well as inner restrictions. Resentment of God can follow, and then the flow of love and life is obstructed. With this example in mind, perhaps Dante's call for zeal can have a deeper meaning: "Oh tarry not: away;" the others shouted; "let time not be lost through slackness of affection;" the others cried, pursuing; "In good work strive, till grace revive from dust!"[6] It is a real risk to think that with resentment and reprisal you can teach life not to treat you any other way than you think you are entitled to. The risk lies in that you may lose contact with your life force and your soul's purpose on Earth. You may feel as if your spirit is killed while you are left to live on.

The effect of this second response is that a more permanent stage of sloth may come into being. We see this in employees who have given up on having any form of ambition. And, regardless of whether it turns into sloth proper or inverted sloth, a number of traits can be distinguished. Characteristic is a lifestyle of going through the motions but not seriously bothering about whether what you feel, say or do accords with your personality or being. It means an inability to be moved by beauty and emotion. It closes the heart to others and so leads to isolation and possible withdrawal from the world. Such withdrawal is also reflected in a closing off of your own potential and talent, which remain underdeveloped and atrophied. It also means that you are not contributing to the growth of the collective, and so others must carry your burden. And you do not care.

One diagnosis that comes close to sloth and zeal is depression. Depression in this context is a way of losing contact with your soul's destiny and will. That what you feel gives real meaning to your life is forgotten or unavailable. Moreover, being hindered from searching for it can also lead to hopelessness and cause much suffering. It is as if you were killing the life within you by not giving it room.

To talk about depression without mentioning the many different forms of depression and the equally frequent methods of treatment, varying from lifelong medication to physical exercises, is a challenge. Suffering in the form of exhausting sadness, mood swings, bipolar disorders, panic attacks, sleeplessness and related symptoms must be differentiated and diagnosed for proper treatment. Each case has a specific pattern that determines the course of therapy. Yet it seems that 80 per cent of prescribed antidepressants are issued by general practitioners who scarcely have sufficient time to investigate the patient's symptoms, sometimes no more than ten minutes.[7] It seems that depression is something we all want to get rid of as quickly as possible.

Leadership development through sloth and zeal

In an ideal world all forms and instances of depression are abnormal and a mood that must be regulated. The reality, though, is that some forms of depression can be symptoms of psychic growth, or in any case change. That is, the depressive feeling, the inability to go on as usual because energy is temporarily unavailable, signals that a new balance is needed in life. From this perspective, depression can be regarded as an attempt by the psyche to create a new balance by incorporating hitherto unconscious potential. When working with clients with this form of life-cycle depression, it is important consciously to articulate that living means more than we can imagine, that is, more than our image of how it is or should be to live. It is counterproductive to too quickly try to run away from it or try to make it go away. There is a saying: "When in the desert don't run too hard to get out." When a new orientation has emerged, then there is energy and life again.

Clients who struggle through these transformations tend to experience a combination of deep feelings of worthlessness about work and a deadness about leisure. There is a profound sense of demystification of life. Everything is merely "nothing but". There are no longer small wonders. Sleeping is difficult, and they cannot recall having dreams. The slothful have not lost their desire for meaning and purpose in life, but the way of acting towards it. They are immobilized by the agony of the interplay between the forces of sloth, desire and apathy. Quite a few leaders experience this almost paradoxical level of activity. On the one hand, they feel immobilized and as if they cannot get anywhere and are not achieving anything. On the other hand, they are so busy and overtaxed that they cannot add one more appointment to their agenda. The loss of meaning relates to this, that nothing they do leads to anything. This is not true because it leads to a lot, especially when it comes to fulfilling tasks. But the point is that it never leads to anything that really matters, because (and this is how they are lazy in a way) they cannot turn all their activity to what really matters to them and shoot with "one bullet", aiming at that. Often this is related to not knowing what really matters to you.

Dreams can be such a treasure in this work. Dreams are the workings of the psyche expressed symbolically on the threshold between conscious and unconscious knowing. They independently reveal something that the ego does not know or understand but needs for the next step. There are many ways to work with dreams. In general you need to pay attention, recall and write down your dreams. One method for paying attention to your dream is to imagine that you are dreaming when you are awake. "If I were to dream . . ." One client who was temporarily caught in sloth and who could not get out of it started an intense series of dreamwork this way. Initially we worked with fairly dull symbols, something like, "Well, I suppose I'm driving my car as usual." Then we would explore them and try to find some associations. This engaged the symbolic thinking and association.

Dante's dream of the Siren is a beautiful example of what dreamwork can do to broaden consciousness. Here is the dream. A woman approaches Dante. She is ugly and deformed. She starts to sing and lures Dante to look at her. In the eyes of Dante she grows irresistible. Another woman appears. She is alarmed at the hypnotic situation Dante is in and cries out to Virgil for help to wake him up. Virgil discloses the Siren and exposes "the ancient witch". Dante wakes up to Virgil's call.

Let us look at how we can understand the relevance of this dream in the context of leadership. First, we must take into account what preceded the dream. Just before falling asleep, Virgil had been telling Dante about love and free will. Dante was thus quite clear in his mind and may have felt that the issues of sloth, zeal, love and free will were resolved. But, nevertheless, the atmosphere of sloth all around him pierced through his bright mind and hooked on to his weakness. He talks about the fancies of his mind (erotic fantasies): "And pleasur'd with the fleeting train, mine eye was clos'd, and meditation chang'd to dream".[8] It has been suggested that because of Dante's emphasis on intellectual knowing here, the woman that meets him in the dream is his unacknowledged feeling side.[9] It is ugly and unattended to, and draws the attention of the dreamer to it. Having no control over the discarded side, feeling turns into fascination, and the more Dante looks at the Siren, the more she appears to be fantastic and beautiful. He projects upon her his ideal self-image, which is not the reality, and that way gets caught in love of a fantasy and not a real person. For a man this is very difficult to break out of. It is significant for a man possessed by a negative anima.[10] The person who saves him from delusion is another woman, one who allies with Virgil, who represents reason. Together they wake Dante up from the lie. The warning woman can be seen as Dante's true instinct and intuition.

What of women? What would be the equivalent of the Siren for a woman? Most likely a woman's gaze would get caught in an image of masculinity, a rigid character with little imagination and low social skills. She would be lured into believing that in order to be successful in a male-dominated world, she would have to be "manly" or emulate male energy. It would be calculated, object and goal oriented, short term, aggressive and judgmental. In the worst case, she would live out that dream and then stop appreciating home, children, nourishing relationships and the value of expressing feelings at work, paired with a permanent focus on what works for now followed by decisions that support it. That would be a woman caught in her negative animus, the inferior man within a woman.

A woman is not a man, and therefore the masculinity of a woman is inferior. By investing libido there instead of in her own nature, she degrades her own femininity and her masculinity as well. A woman can incorporate what we call male energy in such a way that it fertilizes her spiritual development, deepens her psychological understanding of relationships and grounds her in womanhood. For a woman not to pay attention to, develop and honor her being as female and developing womanliness, especially at work and in a leadership role where women are so underrepresented, is an example of sloth; to do so is a real contribution to a better balanced world.

Reflections on zeal

Dirk-Jan van den Berg

For over 30 years I've found myself in a variety of leadership roles, and they've all landed on my path by accident, as life tends to go. Early on, I worked as a government economist, then served as Secretary General in the Ministry of Foreign Affairs for more than eight years. In 2001, I became the Dutch Ambassador to the United Nations in New York. This was my chief learning experience, and an incredibly rich one, together with my stay in China, as the Ambassador of the Netherlands to the People's Republic of China.

What impressed me so much during my years at the UN was that everyone had zeal; we were committed to making the most of our individual roles through genuine collaboration. We worked together in the most rich, diverse context imaginable: people from all over the world contributing intelligence, experience, thoughtfulness and openheartedness. It was fantastic to experience the open flow and stream of ideas that kept everyone motivated and sharp.

Why diversity works

The open flow and rich context of the UN profoundly impacted my role as President of the Executive Board at Delft University of Technology. During my tenure I focused on international exchange, both in research as well as education. Of course, internationalization was not new to Delft, but we were successful in bringing Delft on board of the European research programs. Also, the foreign student community grew in size considerably. These developments require diverse leadership, and I appointed four female directors in the university's support services, as well as three female deans out of eight in total. This was new in the male-dominated world of engineers.

These changes provided valuable interaction, stimulation and inspiration and helped us excel. For example, I hosted regular thematic lunches for diverse groups of employees throughout the organization, organized town hall meetings and communicated through vlogs.

An important condition for diversity is that it must be reflected in multiple ways: gender, age, skills, expertise, visions, orientations . . . This makes "managing the process" interesting and creates space for spontaneity, for something truly new and potentially visionary.

True diversity matters

In my current role at Sanquin I have continued in the same spirit. Diversity is essential. It relaxes the atmosphere and stimulates better, broader thinking and expression. So, I was very pleased to appoint a female colleague in our board, already quite soon after my arrival.

It's also important to me to spend time with the younger generation, one of the key takeaways of my experience at Delft – Generation Z. I truly enjoy learning about their perspectives. What has taken me a long career to discover, they have grown up with: cooperation, communication, transparency, social incentives.

They want to make a contribution to something bigger, and see the blood bank as doing this: Sanquin saves lives. This means that although our salaries are slightly below average, the company atmosphere and purpose aligns with their priorities and offers them the meaning they seek.

I also make a point of personally interacting with external stakeholders including government bodies and donors. It's exciting to facilitate cooperation between so many internal parties: the blood bank, our pharmaceutical company, our research, our diagnostic lab, and Sanquinnovate, our innovation platform.

The Dutch challenge

The Netherlands has historically had a fairly egalitarian wage system. Nevertheless, wealth distribution is a key issue here, as it is globally. For instance, how can we bridge the divide between reward for capital and labor wages which has only increased in recent years? How do we deal with increasing digitalization and its impact on the labor market? We must talk about this openly.

Large groups are feeling resentment and disengagement with society, but complacency is also rife – maybe the two go together? In the

West, we tend to take important things for granted: affordable health-care, a clean environment, no war, inexpensive education, functioning infrastructure, good food. But these important things don't just occur by themselves. And we all have our share of individual responsibility.

Are the politicians to blame?

The political class is confronted with ever increasing complexities and consequently fails to properly address multiple objectives at the same time. Factual investigation and debating differing options are absolutely essential if we are to make informed choices. There are no single solutions to complex problems.

Current political discourse frames multilateral institutions like the UN as bureaucratic with little to no power to change the world. Multilateral institutions are simply not *en vogue* at the moment. It's unfortunate because multilateral exchange is critical to open debate, to identify the critical issues, not to mention international trade.

New laws, rules and regulations create an image of control, however in our complex societies they are doomed to fall short of expectations. This is one of the reasons why so many, and such large, groups of people do not feel represented by their elected officials today. And as a consequence, those politicians who voice discontent are successful, despite a lack of great ideas or inspiring vision.

Learning as a leader

Like many other leaders, I have gone through an "on the job" learning process. At the outset, my mindset was very much hierarchical: I felt responsible for everything and wanted to do my best in every way to be a useful leader for the company, its people and its clients.

Gradually I realized that leading without fully utilizing colleagues' expertise and experience is illusionary. Through interaction and dialogue, forming a vision for the way forward becomes a participatory process. This in turn creates a sense of involvement, importance and belonging. It means not simply collecting individual ideas, but allowing for one whole idea to emerge and moving forward with it together.

This process is extremely inspiring, joyful and beneficial for all involved. This realization prompted a big shift in my focus in terms of leadership: from one to many. The pyramid I had known was turned upside down.

The issue of responsibility in leadership remains potent: who is ulti-mately responsible for the vision, and putting it into action? How does this play out in relation to supervisory board members? These questions are in the process of being addressed. There is no single answer as to how to best regulate and oversee complex networks of co-creativity.

My vision for leadership

Conceptualization has become central to leadership for me. It boils down to four essential questions. First, I take time to address that timeless existential query: why am I here? Next, I look at the produce, the purpose and the environment. Third, I start looking for answers as to direction and strategy. What are the challenges and how can these be met? Finally, I start shaping an agenda focused on actionables, to share with all employees and stakeholders to further define together. What do we want? How can we make it happen?

Experience has taught me when I have struck on something, when it "comes to me" intuitively, with insight and certainty. And I've noticed a tendency in myself to become more relaxed about sharing what is discussed in board meetings. This openness rewards the board as well as the wider company – it creates an atmosphere of trust and inclusion.

What leadership means to me

Leadership is a mission, and absolutely requires zeal. It's not an ego exercise. It's never about you as an individual – it's about what you contribute to a larger purpose. I feel an increasing urgency to create new platforms to facilitate interaction and inspiration. As a leader, I have always sought to offer inspiration, comfort and guidance. To offer a deeper sense of value that I believe matters today, perhaps more than ever.

Notes

1 See Seemiller, C. and Grace, M. (2018). *Generation Z: A Century in the Making*. Oxon: Routledge.
2 Alighieri, D. (1955). *The Divine Comedy II: Purgatory*. Translation by Dorothy L. Sayers. London: Penguin Classics, p. 209.
3 Alighieri, D. (1955). *The Divine Comedy II: Purgatory*. Translation by Dorothy L. Sayers. London: Penguin Classics, p. 209.
4 Jung (1966a), para. 194.
5 Jironet, K. (2009). *Sufi Mysticism into the West: Life and Leadership of Hazrat Inayat Khan's Brothers 1927–1967*. Leuven: Peeters.
6 Alighieri, D. (2004). *The Divine Comedy II: Purgatory*, Canto XVIII: 103–105. Translation by the Rev. H.F. Cary, M.A. Urbana, IL: Project Gutenberg. Retrieved 5 June 2019 from www.gutenberg.org/ebooks/8795.

7 See, for example, Dehue, T. (2009). *De Depressie-Epidemie*. Groningen: Uitgeverij Augustus.
8 Alighieri, D. (2004). *The Divine Comedy II: Purgatory*, Canto XVIII: 143–144. Translation by the Rev. H.F. Cary, M.A. Urbana, IL: Project Gutenberg. Retrieved 5 June 2019 from www.gutenberg.org/ebooks/8795.
9 Luke (1989), p. 83.
10 For a man like Dante who must be considered to have had a fairly well integrated female side, the challenge is perhaps even greater than for a man who has never contemplated feelings, relatedness and nurturing relationships with the intent of integrating such values consciously. In general, when one is on the cusp of a new developmental step, the challenge comes. It is then we are tested and measured before moving on. The more developed we are, the more challenging the test is, and from this perspective it does not get easier because we grow and develop.

Chapter 7

Greed, charity and prudence

Greed, or avarice, is the need to acquire money, material wealth and a position in power structures based on wealth. In the 1990s we experienced an unprecedented acceleration of possibilities to earn material wealth. We were caught up in it, and "more" was regarded as a constant factor; experts envisioned a permanent growth of scale measured in percentages. In 2008 and the aftermath of the largest financial crisis since the 1930s, we started to ask why we think like that, and why governments and financial institutions operated on this assumption? Or, in Alan Greenspan's words to the US Senate:

> Why did corporate governance checks and balances that served us reasonably well in the past break down? At root was the rapid growth in stock market capitalizations in the latter part of the 1990s that arguably engendered an outsized increase in opportunities for avarice. An infectious greed seemed to grip much of our business community.[1]

The idea that everyone can become "president" – rich, famous, influential and a powerful decision maker – is a childish fantasy that has to be outgrown at a time when civilization is making a forward leap to a different level of consciousness, because this notion is just not true.

Such a wake-up call is what most of us (like Dante) encounter in midlife,[2] if not before. Today it looks as if the whole Western world is having a "midlife" crisis. Western civilization is about to emerge from its belief that money is the way to happiness, that it is "good to be greedy", as stated by Ivan Boesky, known for his corporate takeovers and charged with massive fraud in the 1980s. Who still remembers Michael Douglas's impersonation, Gordon Gekko, in the original *Wall Street* film, preaching ". . . The point is, ladies and gentlemen, that greed, for lack of a better word, is good. Greed is right. Greed works. Greed clarifies, cuts through and captures the essence of the evolutionary spirit." Until recently our society held on to the idea that material wealth was associated with happiness, and we were acquiring material objects as totems of happiness to an obscene extent. More than three and a half decades after the release of the original *Wall Street*, we have a more differentiated view on the benefits of greed – good for what? Growth of what? Is growth of capital at the expense of resources *growth*? And is charity its opposite? How can leaders contribute to the shift in consciousness that will lead to a new understanding of wealth?

What we knew all along has now been established by studies in the field of so-called happiness economics. These studies show that beyond providing a basic level of material comfort, more wealth does not create greater happiness. What we are witnessing today is exactly what Dante wrote about. It is a situation in which you cannot keep it together any longer, and you see how everything you built up is disappearing, and it seems you have nothing anymore.

Greed and charity in Dante's Purgatory

It is broad daylight when Dante and Virgil come to the fifth level and meet the greedy. They lie stretched out, weeping, hands and feet fettered, with their faces turned towards the ground and their backs towards Heaven. Their sighing and lamenting are so loud that Dante must sharpen his ears to hear their prayer – what is it about? "My soul cleaves to the dust," they say. It is about the inordinate concern for material things. Greed (*avaritia*) is an excess of materialism at the expense of spiritual matters. All their life energies had been invested in the excessive love of earthly wealth and power, in hoarding and spending. The greedy ones are confronted with their possessive love for earthly material possessions, or, as in the example of Pope Adrian V, in ambition for position and power, which is also completely earthbound. As Dante kneels in reverence to the pope, his shift from greedy grasping to humble sharing is illustrated, and Dante is thus reprimanded: "brother! upon thy feet; Arise: err not: thy fellow servant I (thine and all others') of one Sovran power."[3]

The level of the greedy is so crowded that Dante and Virgil cannot make their way along the outer edge, but must pass between the bodies and the inner side of the cliff. They meet Hugh Capet, who was the first king of France but who now denounces the House of Capet and his sons, the kings who followed him. Their excessive greed for worldly position and wealth had grown fiercely, accompanied by increasing cruelty, theft, betrayal, bribery, manipulation and violence. Hugh Capet named no fewer than seven examples of greed. These are mythological, biblical and classical Roman examples of its various manifestations and downfall. As Dante and Virgil move on, the mountain suddenly shakes, as from an earthquake. But the mountain is not susceptible to such natural phenomena, and Dante is perplexed, absorbed in pondering what it may mean, when he hears "Gloria in excelsis Deo" all around him. Glory to God, the highest, was sung by the angels at the birth of Christ. Here it announces that a soul is free to leave Purgatory and make its final ascent to Heaven. It is the poet Statius who, after 500 years among the greedy, has been released from Purgatory. How was he freed? Statius says that although it may sound amazing, the soul is freed by its own will:

"When any spirit feels itself
So purified, that it may rise, or move
For rising, and such loud acclaim ensures.
Purification by the will alone
Is prov'd, that free to change society
Seizes the soul rejoicing in her will."[4]

Statius continues to explain that of course the soul always wants to move on and leave Purgatory behind, but it cannot will it until the time is right and "ready". "Propension now as eager to fulfil Th' allotted torment, as erewhile to sin."[5] Helen Luke, referring to this important notion, points at something that most of us who have engaged in personal development have encountered – the sudden relief from an old pattern that is as convincing and profound as is the recognition of our unfinished business; that is to say, energy is absorbed by tension until it is resolved and we know and accept it. "However great our desire for it, the will does not really *want* freedom until we have borne the tension and the conflict long enough to purge us of all demand for this or that."[6]

Statius, the poet, had been a strong admirer of Virgil and built his work on the *Aeneid*. Not knowing that he was standing before Virgil, he expresses one wish, which is that he could once meet Virgil. Dante, although warned by Virgil's glance, cannot refrain from smiling, and has to explain that his guide is none other than Virgil. Statius immediately bows to kiss Virgil's feet, but is stopped by Virgil, who says: "Brother! do it not: Thou art a shadow, and behold'st a shade."[7] This being the second instance of correcting veneration on this level, it seems that it is a matter of interest to Dante and to the penance for greed. My understanding is that Dante emphasizes equality; the vision of man as an equal brother or sister, that from a spiritual perspective, none of us can be more or less than we are in relation to each other. We cannot gather or give more than that. If we try, then we will be hoarding or wasting in our relationships and our lives.

Greed is expiated by being bound to Earth, unable to move or see beyond the dust. Also, the penalty for this sin is the way through the sin. It is in experiencing what it means to have turned one's back on the non-material spiritual world while being entirely mired in the earthbound, finite, material side of life. It means longing for the rejected side and for moderation.

The angel of charity erases the fifth "P" on Dante's forehead and says the beatitude that releases him from both greed and prodigality: "Blessed are they who . . . thirst after righteousness." The complete beatitude would read "Blessed are they who hunger and thirst after righteousness," but, as "hunger" is dealt with on the next level, it is omitted here.

Personal developmental aspects of greed and charity: greed and prudence

Greed is the insatiable desire to acquire wealth and possessions beyond what is actually needed. The American psychologist Erich Fromm wrote: "Greed is a bottomless pit which exhausts the person in an endless effort to satisfy the need without ever reaching satisfaction."[8] Typical of greed is that it does not stop, because it never leads to a sense of satisfaction. Once a specific goal has been attained, a new acquisition or ambition surfaces in an everlasting chase. Greed operates at the expense of the needs of others. It often involves using wealth to gain power over others by denying others wealth or power.

Psychologically, greed is an automatic response to the danger of annihilation, a fear of not having an existence. As long as we believe that our existence is a purely material thing, we will overeat, overindulge and overspend. This makes us feel alive; in fact, from this materialistic viewpoint, we prove that we live when we engage in greed. If, on the other hand, we believe that we are entirely nonmaterial and only seek solace in the spiritual abode, then that is a manifestation of the same greed. In this case, it is nurtured by the fear of letting go of the ego, the false self.[9] It is the false self that greedily hungers for "spirituality" and fantasizes about being so highly evolved that the material does not count in life. But no person living is above or beyond being human, and thus of Earth, and so fully immersed in a material existence that cannot be denied. Each of these ways of greed, in their own way, misplaces the center, and creates a lack of balance.

Greed serves to accumulate all that seems valuable to the ego, and makes the ego the center of all efforts. In this way the ego, or the false self in spiritual terms, becomes the one you aim to please, converting you into your own object of worship, or god, if you will. This gives a tremendous sense of being in control and feeling safe. That is what it is all about – are you covered, do you feel safe or not safe? But are you happy when you are "safe"? Is that really effective?

When it comes to greed, it is interesting to note that it is a kind of "double sin". Greed has, as we have seen, two forms of manifestation: hoarding, the closed fist, and prodigality, the open fist, reckless spending. The open fist has in fact caused much distress. Think of all those who have been "out shopping" and come home with things they do not need while incurring credit card debts they cannot pay. Both accumulating and spending lead to decline. Nevertheless, these two principles are the very fundamentals of capitalist economy, the factors that generate its growth. Let us look for a moment at the challenges of growth and what that can mean psychologically in the context of greed.

In the Netherlands, and probably in most of Europe, it is not uncommon for parents to work and save so their children can have a better life. Generation X witnessed grandparents who would not buy a new kitchen pan because that would be a waste since they expect to die soon, and it would be better for the money to go straight to the inheritance. They were striving to create better conditions for the next generation. Is that possible? Or is this a misconception, possibly founded on the dream of eternal life, a better life indeed, and, eventually, victory over dire circumstances – through the children? Psychologically, can you "give" something to another and thereby ensure the betterment of their lives?

In actual fact more often than not reality shows the opposite. Children with huge or medium sized inheritances do not prosper. Instead, they often regress to an earlier, more rudimentary level of development, ethical and otherwise. Rather than the wished for furthering of opulence, it is quite common for children to betray what the parents struggled to achieve. They do so not only by going through the capital, but also by ruining the work ethic and humility that was earned by such struggle.

Every child has the right and the privilege of growth, that is, to work their way out of and beyond whatever level of consciousness the parents developed, despite the inheritance. Such despoiling of wealth and sophistication is often looked upon as immoral and a tragedy, whereas the real tragedy would be the inhibition of growth by stagnation and repetition of parental patterns. So the collective rebuke can be regarded as an instinctive and greedy wish to preserve the existing power structure and, moreover, to make history through future generations. This is greed beyond plain materialism. Psychologically, we realize that greed is far more than materialistic: it loses the real measure of things. It separates possessions from real needs and confuses it with the notion of "value", ultimately with the value you have as a person. The core of greed is possessiveness without measure.

As for the individual, a similar "inheritance" principle applies. Let us say that you are successful and earn a fortune by using one of your talents. The risk is then inevitably that you fall into a pattern of overdoing what you are good at.[10] Not only will you work until you can no longer practice that talent, but, and this is more serious, you do not develop other potentials within yourself. Let us say that your preferred talent is in extraverted, social networking, and that you earn your position, wealth and future career opportunities by doing just that. You have no time for your introverted, homebound base, and it has no space to grow, see e.g., Michelle Obama's autobiography, *Becoming* (2018). Not only will this make you one-sided, but the undeveloped side may eventually take its place and "ruin" what you built up. We typically see this in burn-outs.

From a psychological perspective, a burn-out can to some extent be likened to what Jung called "loss of soul". Loss of soul, then, means a condition characterized by lack of energy, little or no sense of orientation or meaning in life, regression, and disintegration of well-known life patterns and consciousness.[11]

Burn-out can also be seen as an impetus for conscious development to seek a harmony between ego and Self. In my experience, burn-out is a chronic state of inner stress that can no longer be balanced with reduced workload or altered activities. The reason is that the inner stress demands a collapse of what has been a renewal of life, but the person suffering from burn-out has no access to the energy required to execute this transition. That sort of energy has simply never been developed. This is further complicated by the conviction that initially gave the impulse to greed, namely, that without material security there is no life. So, by holding on to "more", what is created in fact is poverty.

This irony is often represented in literature – Charles Dickens' Scrooge, Thomas Hardy's John D'Urberville, and William Shakespeare's King Lear are but a few examples of characters full of greed. Kino, the young pearl diver in John Steinbeck's *The Pearl*, finds the pearl of the world and becomes so attached to it that he proclaims, "This pearl has become my soul, if I give it up I shall lose my soul" (1994: 28). Obviously, the moral (one of many in *The Pearl*) is that the reverse is rather the case: if he keeps the pearl he loses his soul; if he lets it go, he saves his soul.

The immense popularity and perseverance of these works point to the universality of the theme of greed and to our collective indignation and disdain. It is very easy, and even sanctioned, to judge greed immediately because it really is not good, unless we consciously work with the inner friction of greed. This is illustrated in the example of Scrooge: striving for possession makes us unfree, it chains us down. And, as Statius taught us, this is why, on the one hand, the greedy are freed by their own free will. On the other hand, we can only be freed from greed when the right time has come. Scrooge realized this: he ran into a dead-end pursuing greed; he is forced to experience its inner friction to its bitter end, and only then does he become capable of freeing himself from it. This is the first true act of free will.

Yet at the same time, although less immediate and often not overtly, we feel compassion for greedy characters. Take, for example, Scrooge, who loses his fiancée for money and terrorizes his clerk Cratchit even at Christmas. We have compassion for him because we notice what greed does to him, we see how his heart becomes cold and closed, we see how more and more becomes less and less. But of what exactly? More isolation and less love.

The treasure of life is in the heart of a person. By that I mean that all the wealth in the world is readily available through happiness, and happiness comes from within, not from external material objects. You can only appreciate the value of these if your heart is open to it. A classic example of this is indeed the Christmas celebration, when you receive an abundance of gifts. Let us say that you did not have a good day, no contact with yourself and no feelings of happiness. Will the present make you happy? No, it will make it worse. It will point straight to the fact that nothing in the world is going to make you happy. Happiness, contentment, safety, warmth, intimacy, union with others, friendship, understanding, kindness – all the different ways of love – emanate from an open heart.

Charity is "love for the other", *agape* in ancient Greek, the true meaning of "love your neighbor as yourself". So, first you love yourself and feel peace and harmony within, then you love your neighbor in that same way. I am aware that this sounds somewhat religious, but I know of no other way of expressing the basic fact that charity comes to a person who not only seeks safety externally, but also exercise reliance on the inner, immaterial, eternal being – the true Self we call the soul – and who sacrifices the false self for it. Sometime in life, perhaps around midlife, we all have the opportunity to realize that this is the only safety there is. That is when charity can be translated into our business practice, in a form of prudence that we will now examine. The choice is yours.

Leadership development through greed and charity: greed and prudence

In Dante's Purgatory, greed is the sin with the greatest repercussions because it impacts the whole of society in its corrupting nature. In a global economy that means all humanity is affected. There is little to add in terms of information, interpretation or perspectives when it comes to the negative effects of greed on the economy and how this reflects on the leadership that has sustained it over the last decades. Bankers' bonuses – by now – there is a final agreement among the world's wealthiest countries to try to regulate such bonuses and an agreement on rebalancing the global economy, with a strong emphasis on fiscal responsibility and structural reforms.

Will that do it? I do not believe so, because I think it is hardly feasible to expect a single leader, or group of leaders, to change the course of greed within the very same system that fostered it, to create real change while tackling the problem with the same techniques as the ones that led to the problem in the first place. More regulations, fewer regulations, no regulations – it is still a matter of how much greed the system can handle. It is for this reason that this is a particularly interesting time of hope, because now there is a window of opportunity that allows an influence outside the system to shift the balance and put us all on a new course.

Melinda Gates, for one, in her candid autobiography shows through lived examples how women networks evolved, grew and gradually changed the culture at Microsoft. Relating one case she describes how this happened:

> When women were wounded, they were able to absorb their pain without passing it on. But when the men, they needed to make someone pay. That's what fed the cycle of war . . . when women gather with one another, include one another, tell our stories to one another, share our grief with one another, we find our voice with one another. We create a new culture – not one that is imposed on us, but one that we build with our own voices and values.[12]

Renunciation of greed that leads to charity is furthered by prudence in leadership practice. Prudence has come to mean "good judgment", and is often used to promote morally correct actions, especially caution, so it has also come to be associated with being overcautious, or cowardliness. But its original meaning was very different, which is typical of all powerful concepts. They are acquired by the power in place, in this case the pope, and then changed to fit the regime. But we can rediscover "prudence" in order to know the value of the knowledge it offers.

In the beginning, prudence was not an activity at all. It was gnosis, the factor behind; it regulated all virtues. What is this gnosis, or knowledge, or wisdom, if you will? Well, nobody can tell for sure because it is not a fixed thing; it is a fluid, clear vision of what each situation holds. Inclusion, multiple views, informal deliberations. It is the kind of open mindedness that recognizes the true variety and complexity of things and situations, and is not caged in any presumption of deceptive knowledge. It does not include "shoulds", musts, and conventional thinking. For instance, telling the truth is not always good. What makes telling the truth a virtue is whether it is done with prudence. The capacity by which prudence operates restores the sacred relationship between earthly matters and formless soul. It shows us time and again that social good is greater than personal possession.

Prudent thinking is rooted in the notion of free will and as such is outrageously independent of the system that binds a person through fear or a false promise of material safety and power. Prudence is the intent to do the right thing, not necessarily to look right.

Leaders now have the chance to establish the new leadership by becoming independent of the old system, the rules of the old economy, and the perks of the old economy. However, it does require strength from within, in fact it requires an extraordinary sense of intellect and purpose to sustain that interiority while taking others' interest into the equation. Choosing to be specific in a group setting is a powerful method for examining terms, concepts and rhetoric that lead towards constructive governance and transparency around diverse groups' interests.

Reflections on charity

Mijntje Lückerath-Rovers

Over the past twenty years as an economist, I've conducted research and published on corporate governance, the representation of women on boards of directors and diversity. The situation – women are underrepresented in top positions – has not significantly changed in that period of time. When it comes to top positions within Dutch companies, gender diversity is extremely low. As the author of *The Dutch Female Board Index* over the past decade, I've followed the topic closely, and have witnessed only minute fluctuations over this time. Among the newly listed companies in 2018, *none* of the board directors appointed were women. Of the 90 companies in the index, still 77 have no female executive directors and 22 have no female non-executive directors. These statistics are astonishing, really, given that there is simultaneously an increasing acceptance of women in leading roles. So, in some ways, nothing has changed.

In other ways, I have recently observed significant change, which has primarily manifested in the form of greater transparency. Non-executive board members with whom I have worked for some time are now showing their commitment and involvement much more tangibly. They also speak far more openly about their personal motivations for fulfilling the role. Things are in essence more personal and visible, and less complex.

The power of definition

Perhaps it is paradoxical, but I believe we are often deluded and distracted by concepts that are either insufficiently clear or too obvious to mean anything substantial. *The Big Short* is an extraordinary film based on the 2008 US financial crisis. One highpoint is the interlaced definition of complex financial instruments such as sub-prime loan or credit default swap. The implication is that these terms are used to covertly describe the actual implications of the instruments. This kind of deceptive branding is potentially dangerous.

It has been argued that if it were "Lehman Sisters" the financial crisis would probably not have happened. One of the chief reasons being that women would not have taken the enormous risks – gambling on gambling with no real product being involved. Another reason frequently mentioned is that women seek to establish unambiguous language. According to Halla Tomasdottir and Kristin Petursdottir – whose bank in Iceland survived the financial crisis without government assistance – the financial world's language needs to be accessible and not strengthening the estranging characteristics of the banking culture.

And yet contemporary jargon is not so very different. Since the Corporate Governance Code was revised in 2016, the corporate governance discourse has been centered around "long-term value creation".[13] But this new buzzword has no clear meaning and in practice many professionals, directors and commissioners seem to find it a "vague principle". This can lead to misunderstandings. As a commissioner I query its true meaning, and how it can become a realistic proposition when multiple, often conflicting values are involved. So, let us have a look at what long-term value creation entails. The new Corporate Governance Code stipulates that long-term value creation is the main objective when drawing up the long-term strategy. But it is also crucial in risk management, when considering the interests of all stakeholders and on topics such as culture and remuneration policy. Of course, the code does not prescribe what this long-term value response is and how you determine it. Supervisory directors and directors of each company must define this themselves, there is no "one size fits all".

A first step towards making long-term value creation more explicit is to make a distinction between economic and social value creation, and within that between internal and external value creation.

Working from within

Internal economic value creation focuses on areas where the company adds financial value to its own business operations. This includes entrepreneurship, innovations, mergers and risk appetite. External economic value creation is related to the added financial value flowing forth from the internal value creation, such as financial performance and shareholder return. Social value creation is related to values and identity and more difficult to measure, although often reflected in the mission: what kind of company do we want to be? The stakeholder model applied in the

Netherlands plays a major role here. Internally, this is reflected for instance in view on employees, on ethical issues and on leadership style. Externally, on the other hand, it aims at broader social issues such as corporate social responsibility, employment in the wider sense, and product quality.

We see these four quadrants picture clearly when a company makes the decision about relocating production to low-wage countries. Relocation may be good from the point of view of cost savings and for the shareholder, but is not favorable for current employees and may not be a good choice from a social perspective either. In addition, directors and supervisory directors do not all have the same priorities in such an assessment. These priorities can differ because everyone, consciously or unconsciously, has a personal preference and perspective, formed by his or her own experiences and interests.

Transparency matters

A second step that is necessary to make long-term value creation explicit: discussing everyone's preferences and priorities with each other. In my experience it is not always easy to realize this step. Because what are you, as a supervisory director or director, willing to relinquish within the set four quadrants of value creation? And what not? An exercise that I have found helpful here is to invite each and every Commissioner or Director to first complete his or her four quadrants individually. When comparing the results, it will soon become clear how many different views coexist, and how vague the concept of long-term value creation is defined. Discussing the preferences and priorities of the individual Supervisory Directors and Directors will ensure that long-term value creation is given concrete meaning and becomes a useful addition to corporate governance.

In the same vein, I also perceive greater accountability. In the process of defining the *long-term value*, for example, boardroom discussions become more outspoken. The big shift here is the increasing trend towards value creation for society, (sometimes described as a feminine positioning, however, that has some stereotyping in it, which I am trying to avoid), which entails taking a broad view on stakeholder perspectives. My contribution is often to consciously hold a different perspective. For example for many companies, the financial performance, including risks and business opportunities, get priority in board meetings. What's not so obvious, yet just as relevant – and sometimes even more interesting – are the inalienable cultural and corporate governance issues that are also important to create long-term value.

Why we need diversity

In my view, the arguments in favor of diversity boil down to two. First, a moral argument – equality is a basic human right. Second, an economic argument – diversity nourishes business. It's common knowledge that monocultures stagnate and perish. IMF research into diversity evidences that having women in leadership positions leads to greater financial stability, lower levels of non-performing loans and higher profits. Obviously, greater diversity means views are more diverse. Diversity is critical to reducing groupthink and to stimulating the meaningful, rigorous discussion required for genuine creativity and better decision-making. Without diversity, organizations will never break through old habits and dusty tradition. This is particularly important given the increase in polarization we are witnessing globally.

The growth of the sisterhood

Another new development is the increasing number of women's and girls' networks. Remember Madeleine Albright's words in 2006: "There is a special place in hell for women who don't help other women." Women in leadership positions did not promote each other, and I think that's different now. I sense a growing sisterhood. Personally, I get a lot out of working and collaborating with women, and also from my friendships with other (business) women. My business friends and I sometimes travel and golf together, and share and support each other. These are valuable experiences and I want to see more of the feminine dynamic, inside and outside the boardroom.

Since I turned 50, I have started looking for more satisfaction in my work. I am seeking to be of relevance on boards that are open to modernization through the creation of transparency, equality, and value – even if only within the given, fixed framework. I find that my entire quality of life has improved significantly thanks to this renewed focus. I'm grateful I have earned the right to make that kind of choice. There is much to be said for the wisdom and perspective experience provides, and a certain confidence that flows as a result.

Notes

1 Testimony of Chairman Alan Greenspan, *Federal Reserve Board's Semiannual Monetary Policy Report to The Congress*, 16 July 2002.
2 Stein, M. (2003). *In MidLife*. Putnam, CT: Spring Publications.

3 Alighieri, D. *The Divine Comedy II: Purgatory*, Canto XIX: 133–135. Translation by the Rev. H.F. Cary, M.A. Urbana, IL: Project Gutenberg. 2004. Retrieved 5 June 2019 from www.gutenberg.org/ebooks/8795.

4 Alighieri, D. *The Divine Comedy II: Purgatory*, Canto XXI: 58–63. Translation by the Rev. H.F. Cary, M.A. Urbana, IL: Project Gutenberg. 2004. Retrieved 5 June 2019 from www.gutenberg.org/ebooks/8795.

5 Alighieri, D. *The Divine Comedy II: Purgatory*, Canto XXI: 67–69. Translation by the Rev. H.F. Cary, M.A. Urbana, IL: Project Gutenberg. 2004. Retrieved 5 June 2019 from www.gutenberg.org/ebooks/8795.

6 Luke (1989), p. 90.

7 Alighieri, D. *The Divine Comedy II: Purgatory*, Canto XXI: 131–132. Translation by the Rev. H.F. Cary, M.A. Urbana, IL: Project Gutenberg. 2004. Retrieved 5 June 2019 from www.gutenberg.org/ebooks/8795.

8 Fromm (1994), p. 115.

9 Winnicott, the pediatrician, psychiatrist, and psychoanalyst, coined the term "false self": "The false self, developed on a compliance basis, cannot attain to the independence of maturity" (1975, p. 225).

10 For a note on the relevance of this to leadership development, see, for example, Kaplan, R.E. and Kaiser, R.B. (2009). Stop Overdoing Your Strengths. *Harvard Business Review*, 87(2): 100–103.

11 C. G. Jung says: "The values which the individual lacks are to be found in the neurosis itself" (1966b, p. 93).

12 Gates (2019), pp. 256–257.

13 For more information, an article in Dutch is available at https://fd.nl/opinie/1279680/lange-termijn-waardecreatie-is-nieuwe-buzzwoord-in-corporate-governance.

Chapter 8

Gluttony and temperance

Gluttony is not glamorous. Compared to the sins we have discussed before, gluttony is by far the least attractive. It has nothing of the glory of pride, or the awesomeness of anger. It does not shine with the strategic brilliance of envy or greed, and cannot compete with the savvy melancholic depression of the slothful. Gluttony is rather associated with animal-like qualities, but then without the sexy beastliness of lust. Gluttony traditionally manifests in eating and drinking, and ends up in heaviness, hangover and the shame of satiation. Gluttony is usually associated with the body, and can also express itself in other forms of consumption, be they material or spiritual. Modern society is riddled with opportunities for gluttony, and temperance has perhaps never been further from the norm.

Gluttony and temperance are most commonly viewed as being about our relationship to food and beverages, to eating and drinking, to tasting and swallowing. Gluttony comes from one of our first, most primary needs in the sense that without nourishment we will die. It focuses on the body, our material well-being, and thereby highlights the trap of mind-body division. But gluttony is not simply an expression of survival instincts and the need for sufficient physical nourishment. It can manifest in too much love for nourishment in a more general sense, for instance, too much love for attention. In all their forms, gluttony and temperance reflect embodiment: how a person lives in the flesh and how they express that, whether in words or images, whether directly, via social media or other means.

The word glutton comes from *gula* – "throat". In the throat are the vocal cords, the glottis. Humans are the only species that communicates through speech and language. The use of language, according to Dante, is subject to scrutiny on this the second highest of terraces. Also today one can observe a correlation between gluttonous eating and gluttonous speaking. Just as the food goes down, so the words come out. Often without attention, distinction or care for the receiving end, be it the palate or someone else's newsfeed. Gluttony manifests in overconsumption, but also in underconsumption. In both cases, the "food" is always the central point of concentration, the thing our attention goes to. Undereating as a manifestation of gluttony is an example of the false virtue, analogous to examples in previous chapters. Just as humbleness can be a cover-up for pride, so can underconsumption be a mask of gluttony.

The lurking sensation that something within us is missing that needs to be filled from the outside, that we are not whole, is prevalent in our society. This sensation is fed and amplified by advertising, and particularly with the enormous growth in time spent online and behind screens, advertising is inescapable.[1] These days, our exposure to advertising is insidious − no longer a 30-minute spot during a television show or a billboard by the freeway, advertisements can be a one-liner in the sidebar of your Facebook newsfeed, or a few seconds of a video clip before you watch something on YouTube.

This driving need to fill the gaps in our inner life by consuming (food, alcohol, drugs, sex, social media, shopping, making a certain figure of money, having a particular number of Instagram followers) inevitably leads to gluttony, because the notion that such gaps can be filled by an external item or experience is fundamentally false. No amount of these external sources will do. These purported means of achieving wholeness will never satiate us, because these gaps can never be filled by the external. This dynamic creates the "insatiable" hunger we are caused to feel, hoping that the next meal, or high, or million, will quiet the voices of discontent. The truth is that those voices do not speak the truth, for in fact we are already whole. The only way to fill the gaps is to understand that *there are no gaps*. This requires us to work on our inner self and come to the deeply held belief that everything we need we already have within: that we are each an intrinsically whole being who is not lacking in any way, and that this has always been the case. Only when this belief is fully instilled does the hunger for external gratification subside. We might still seek out and enjoy pleasure, but we understand that it has no correlation with a sense of completeness and finality. Gluttony believes there is not enough for everyone. Temperance trusts in abundance.

Food and beverage have symbolic value, which provides meaning to various situations. We appreciate foods and manners in their contexts. In this way, there is a difference between eating at an excellent restaurant, eating at home alone or eating at a sports event. In our culture, where food is abundant, gluttony is linked to food largely in a symbolic relation. This can lead to the superficial use of food as an object and a substitute for things that food was not intended for. Food and drink become objects that must fill emptiness and cover for lack of enjoyment. In addition, this consumption does indeed divert attention from other things, any communion beyond the actual eating.[2]

Similarly, in our culture, there is an abundance of means for communication, which puts more pressure on the use of language. Being able immediately to reach a person, or a large group of people, in another geography, for instance via social media, increases demand on the sender's ability to interact without non-verbal cues or simultaneously to address a variety of people without offending a single individual. As we well know, language is not always used considering this. Verbal abuse is a form of gluttony that affects not only the glutton, but also other people, the recipients. Cyberbullying, electronic, mostly anonymous, posting of negative messages about a person, is widespread – more than 30 per cent of teens have been reported to have experienced it.[3]

Temperance, the virtue that accompanies gluttony, means that primary attention goes to things other than eating, drinking and attention. This occurs naturally when we are neither too hungry nor too full. Temperance teaches us precisely how to not indulge in either of these states, and so facilitates the movement of consciousness to other realms than the purely carnal. Temperance offers guidance in our decisions around our online presence, and how to find balance between harnessing the benefits of the Internet and our online lives, while finding the requisite discipline to disconnect from the online when it transmutes from meaningful into distractive, wasteful or harmful. Where do we draw the line between online behavior that facilitates connection, inspiration and creativity, and that which detracts from our focus, or compromises our sense of peace and inner confidence? It is a balance that can take time to strike, and in the course of doing so we will need to set, reset and fiercely guard our boundaries.[4]

In language and speech, temperance manifests in different forms of respect. In a diverse business community, it is critical that leaders develop temperance in the ways in which they do, or opt not to, behave and communicate. Online, rather than face-to-face, communication is an evolving art.

Gluttony and temperance in Dante's Purgatory

The poets arrive at the sixth level. Turning right, they come upon a big tree that seems to grow upside down. The tree is watered by a sparkling cascade and full of delicious fruits. Dante is startled by the vision, and thinks the tree must be growing this way so that nobody can climb it. Then they hear a voice from within the tree that forbids them to eat the fruit. It continues speaking and gives examples of temperance, mentioning first the Virgin Mary who, rather than stilling her own hunger at the marriage in Cana, took care of the guests to make the marriage worthy and complete. The voice proceeds by naming the noble ladies of Rome, who according to custom did not drink wine, but instead chose water. The third example is Daniel, who rejected the king's food and wine to seek wisdom. The fourth was the delight in simplicity at a time before cooking and winemaking introduced people to gluttonous feasting. Finally, fifth, the voice speaks of John the Baptist, who lived on honey and locusts in the desert and thereby earned the glory that the Gospel demonstrates.

As Dante continues to peer into the tree to try to find out who is speaking there, Virgil calls upon him to move on. They are soon caught up by a group of the gluttonous, starved as they are, purging from overeating, their countenances so emaciated and bony that the words "Omo dei" (man is of God) can be read in their faces.[5] As they are coming up from behind, Dante hears:

'My lips,
O Lord!' and these so mingled, it gave birth
To pleasure and pain.[6]

The prayer of the gluttonous, "Lord, open my lips," and it continues, "and my mouth shall show forth Thy praise." The prayer is a reminder that the mouth is there also to express veneration for the beauty of the sublime being, the creator of all. Gluttony (*gula*) is misplaced longing to praise that life force. When eating and drinking, gulping down the spirit replaces consciousness of that creating life force, gluttony dulls a person. That is why the penance of the gluttonous is starvation. They are prevented from eating in the face of abundance. Hence the tree with its fragrant fruit that is out of reach.

As the gluttonous pass, Dante hears a familiar voice, and after a while recognizes Forese Donati, an old friend. Forese tells Dante about how he "followed appetite to excess" on Earth, eating and drinking without measure, and how he is now starving. Dante is astonished to find Forese so high up the mountain at the sixth level. Having just learned about "time" and the long time Statius had to spend on the level of sloth, why is it that Forese, only five years after his death, was already here? It was because of his wife, Forese explained, who had had such power of love and prayer that she had assured his swift movement to Heaven. This example of selfless love and generosity of a woman towards her husband, even when he is already dead, fits the level of gluttony. It points beyond starvation: *vocal articulation* directed towards the only power, God. Intense prayer for another, for a loved one, is a way of acknowledging that there is something beyond ourselves. Therefore, it also has an effect that goes beyond life on Earth. At the same time, it is interesting to note that Forese, who had neglected his wife when he lived with her, now gives full tribute to her, and so heals his heart by opening it to his love for her.[7]

As we see, for Dante gluttony is symbolically concerned not only with digestion and absorption, but also with expression. Gluttony in its immediate form is about overeating or undereating, what we consume to sustain life. But symbolically, as in the case of Forese and the prayer of the gluttonous, we see that gluttony can also apply to different levels of the conscious use of verbal expression. It is an effect of temperance to discipline our speech. Temperance leads us into awareness of the intent behind our use of words. This is an important lesson on the sixth level.

Temperance teaches us how to seek satisfaction for the things we want and need, but to do so with a conscious mind and with alertness and presence of being. To restrain gluttony, the mind must be directed to something that goes beyond the need and the object of need, even if it is the fruit of knowledge, and thus concentrate it on the creator of both hunger and the stilling of it. This is what makes a person balanced and fit. In one of the examples given as an illustration of temperance from the Old Testament, Gideon led his troops to drink at the river and observed which of them remained alert despite their thirst and so scooped up the water and lapped it from their hands, and who simply knelt and gulped down the water directly from the stream, thereby abandoning every form of precaution. Gideon then picked the 300 who had remained watchful and maintained their soldierly quality by lapping the water, and advanced only with them to victory.

When the Angel of Temperance brushes off the sixth "P" from Dante's forehead, he hears the benediction:

> And then a voice: "Blessed are they, whom grace
> Doth so illume, that appetite in them
> Exhaleth no inordinate desire,
> Still hung'ring as the rule of temperance wills."[8]

To shift the direction of hunger from food to righteousness means that all hunger is within measure. The mastering of gluttony sets a person free from cravings in general. That is why it is a relief when consciousness moves out of the strictly carnal domain. This is the work of temperance.[9]

The appearance of the angel is so fierce and powerful that Dante is completely blinded. This indicates the force by which such measure is demanded, possibly also in anticipation of the challenges at the next level of the lustful. But most of all, the Angel of Temperance is gentle. Dante's description of its gentleness offers such a beautiful feeling of the softness of the Angel of Temperance: "such a wind I felt upon my front blow gently, and the moving of a wing perceiv'd, that moving shed ambrosial smell."[10] It reminds me of Sufi poetry describing the presence of God as a fragrance, as the gentlest touch to the nostrils of the fragrance of roses. Anyone approaching food and beverage under this influence surely does so in the most gracious way.

Personal developmental aspects of gluttony and temperance

As discussed above, gluttony is the sin that only wants to swallow and to overindulge. It manifests either as insatiable hunger or a desire for starvation. It means that you either want more and more or nothing. These are motivations different from the desire for control that we find among the prideful. For the gluttonous, the intake of food and attention represents a symbolic lifeline. For a gluttonous person to feel in control of this lifeline and its key to nourishment is a triumph in being able to consume as much or as little as desired. What these two ways have in common is the excess of need for control of nourishment. It is therefore interesting that the virtue that goes with gluttony is temperance, because temperance also entails self-control. The difference, though, is that temperance fosters balance rather than excess. On this level too, the sin and the virtue go hand in hand.

All times and cultures are likely to have had ideal images of beauty that women tried to emulate. Significant for our beauty ideal is precisely its focus on the physical, the preponderance of the bodily appearance. This is especially true for the ideal image of women's bodies.

Body weight and shape are central to our ideal image of the body. These factors are to a large extent regulated by a combination of our intake of food and beverages and how much we exercise. It is from the perspective of an ideal physical form and the image we present to the world that we must try to understand the dynamics of perfection and control that signify gluttony and temperance today. We see this clearly in the pathological struggles related to anorexia nervosa, bulimia nervosa and binge eating disorder, which have in common the desire for control and perfection. These are very serious conditions that cannot easily be treated. They mainly affect women between the ages of 15 and 30, but approximately 10 per cent are men. Eating disorders are linked to shame. They are the diagnoses with the highest level of suicide, and the mortality rate in the Netherlands is approximately 6 per cent.[11]

Doctors talk about low self-esteem as being one of the important reasons for eating disorders. It may well be that the ideal image of the woman presented by mass media prompts frantic dieting. It is however a misunderstanding to link body culture, with its fame, success and vast amounts of money, directly to eating disorders. Not all people who diet do so to boost self-esteem and confidence. Not all people who diet to improve their appearance suffer from an eating disorder. But indirectly there is an association because the ideal image of a woman's body is linked to the much deeper notion of beauty. Moreover, if you remove the layer of glamour associated with the beauty industry, you see a much more serious conception. What of eating and the relationship to yourself? Eating patterns can reflect your mental state to outside observers. I once heard of a psychiatrist in Zurich who treated clients who had a great a variety of symptoms and complaints. There were times when he could not easily get to the core of a patient's condition. He would then ask that patient to have lunch with him. During their meal the picture would become clearer, and he could proceed to form a diagnosis and plan a treatment procedure. Many psychiatric patients eat without any contact whatsoever with the world around them. They also do not always notice what they eat. Sometimes we are all like that.

Eating – what you select to eat, how you tackle the food, how you put it into your mouth (little or much; beginning of the mouth or far in towards the glottis), level of attention when chewing, duration of mastication, swallowing, interval before this whole process is repeated in the next bite, in conjunction with your use of beverages, or not, and so on – shows how you relate to yourself at that moment.

Thomas Aquinas elaborated the list earlier created by St. Gregory the Great and defined six ways to commit gluttony: eating too soon, too expensively, too much, too eagerly, too daintily and eating wildly. I think we can say that the same goes for drinking. Today there is an abundance of advice on all this and extensive information about what is good for us in terms of eating and drinking. It is likely that education has helped prevent many people from dying young by advocating low-cholesterol diets, "dry days" in the week, and exercise. But that is not the point here. The point is that despite education, the inclination to approach food and drink remains much the same. They reflect the relationship you have with yourself. What is the reason? One reason I have discovered while working with people in leadership roles is that gluttony is linked to extreme and constant stress. The problem of stress does not emanate from a sequence of laborious activities with a predetermined set of steps and actions. No, it is the anguish that comes from not knowing where to begin.

The disconnection of body from Self that is so prevalent in social media culture takes this form under the influence of excessive demands at work; it creates a rift in the connection between physical and spiritual nourishment. The body and the mind disconnect, which in turn causes a state of permanent stress.[12] This boils down to an endless, insatiable hunger for attention.

In our modern world, it is all too easy to become gluttonous for attention, where the endless realm of the Internet forms our stage. Thousands of people around the globe suffer from "social media anxiety disorder",[13] yet we cannot seem to stop ourselves from succumbing to the addictive nature of social media. Seeking attention and external validation through social media is now considered quite normal, particularly for younger generations, with children as young as eight owning smartphones and having their own (presumably monitored) social media accounts. Some use the platforms as a way of keeping in touch with others; some cast a wider net, hoping to become an "influencer" and even make money from their image. Either way, the image(s) we present are inevitably a cultivated version of our lives, and every single thought or picture shared has a motivation behind it, positive or negative. We seek to be perceived in a particular way – generally as successful, whatever our definition of this term might be – and this urge now pulses through us multiple times per day. Social interaction no longer entails getting dressed and going out to meet someone – it's as simple as reaching for your cell phone. The threshold is lower, which makes it all the easier to overconsume and succumb to gluttony.

Throwaway lines such as "if it's not on social media, it didn't happen" are only a half-joke: we experience anxiety when our attractive, filtered adventures are not online and ready for consumption. Our ego readily becomes very attached to the image we cultivate, and we can attach vastly excessive importance to how our image is received and responded to by others. Appearance and image, as well as the vast changes in travel and the global reach of the Internet, have drastically shifted how we perceive ourselves, how we consume and how we (in the form of our online image) are consumed. In the space of a few generations, photography has gone from being a special and expensive affair, done by a qualified professional in a studio, to something that everyone with a smartphone can do. The phenomenon of selfies, and the many filters, apps and programs that can be used to "correct" our appearance, together with social media platforms to display ourselves, means that we consider ourselves (i.e. our external selves) to be our own brands. Whether our brand is successful depends on how many likes we get (and who does the liking), how many followers we derive and how the image is received by others. We measure our self-worth by how much approval we gain from the online world, rather than knowing ourselves to be intrinsically worthy. This schism makes it difficult to detach ourselves from the potentially powerful hold social media can have over our identity and our ego.

Leadership development through gluttony and temperance

Particularly in the context of leadership, our hunger for attention, approval and validation can be detrimental, because when this form of gluttony manifests, nothing will satisfy it, because it is a misplaced longing for the infinite that has been misdirected to finite sources. Gluttony for attention is a manifestation of a person's longing for self-esteem. What cannot be experienced internally is sought from external sources. Just as our culture's fixation on the body leads to a wish for a figure that can never be perfect enough, corporate cultures tend to abuse our need for attention. It is a kind of anorectic situation, typical of gluttony, in which underattention results in overperformance.

Temperance in Dante's Purgatory is much more than being able to say stop to gluttonous cravings. Temperance is about how much you can remember to value yourself, irrespective of others, and how much you honor the life force within that makes you the unique being you are.

Reflections on temperance

Michiel Le Comte

I have worked in the financial services industry for 20 years, in fields including private banking, asset management and insurance. Over the past decade, I've served as a supervisor at the Dutch Central Bank. The DCB has a different role to a commercial bank – it's not meant to be profitable. So, the focus is on what we contribute to society, not what we get out of it. I like that idea.

My version of leadership

I don't feel as though I work for a "company", but for a boss who has a vision that resonates with what I believe in and what I want to be part of. That inspiration creates an exciting and joyful setting, for which the company is a vessel. I avoid emphasizing my leadership role because my effectiveness is not a result of my function, but my knowledge, expertise, experience and personality. I aim to create space for finding solutions, especially when things go wrong. Sure, I challenge my team, but only to a certain point. There must always be room for whatever is needed.

In leading my team I've made a conscious decision to be transparent about what I believe in, how that impacts my daily life, what I do and say, and what I value in others and our relationship. I tend to be sensitive to the quality of the energy in my team. I strive to steer towards what can best be described as flow. It is a state of mind in which all feel included and appreciated. Things move easily. It's enjoyable. I reach this by talking about the priority of imparting energy to your colleague. I also challenge pre-existing ideas by talking about the present, bringing them into the here and now. Paradoxically, that is often where the great unknown lies. For me, metaphors are powerful images that stay with people, not due to the content, but because of how it made them feel.

Freedom and listening

Temperance is about process, not the end goal. And contentment is a consequence of temperance. If it were up to me, I'd abolish performance management, because the focus is misguided. Its implementation leads to depreciation of talent, and the system of external gratification and attention is outdated.

Imagine you have to commit to performance goals that will be assessed at the end of the year, and you will be measured as to whether you have achieved these or not. Would you aim for the moon? Most people do not. Instead, they fabricate targets that are reachable with limited effort and, especially, low risk. It's such a waste of talent, resources, spirit, and goals that could have been met in a more free and balanced environment, allowing for experimentation within limits.

We need to listen and inquire. I've experienced many times how a boring meeting can be altered into a vibrant one, simply by listening, giving attention and asking questions. We all have a responsibility to not allow the usual suspects to ramble on, not as a confrontation, but through attention.

The pitfalls of the digital realm

While the Internet offers tremendous, unparalleled benefits, it is also the greatest "time-sink". Everything associated with "digital" stimulates a chase, a search for short-term gratification. It is a medium designed to capture attention, but not to sustain it. Its high pace impacts attention span negatively. A tsunami of short texts trigger expectations on "delivery", and create longing for satisfaction that's never met.

Research in neuropsychology shows how these stimuli are associated with excitation of dopamine. In an experiment, a mouse was presented with a lever that it could press any time to release dopamine to its brain. It forsook eating and drinking for that stimulus – there was never enough. It shows the addictive potential of everything from games to "breaking news". To be a selective user requires sustained self-control.

Abstinence works for me. I'm not on Facebook, Twitter or other social media, so I don't expose myself to the exhausting challenge of constantly choosing. Meditation is a helpful practice that facilitates the choice to stay out of the cycle of instant gratification.

My personal daily practice

When I was younger, I practiced martial arts for my physical, mental and spiritual development. After leaving, I stayed in touch with my peers and one of my classmates was practicing a form of Buddhism called Samatha, to which he introduced me. It is a form of Theravada Buddhism, which aims at calming the mind through concentration practices.

I practice "sounding", repeating the same sound or mantra for 20 minutes, at home each day. I also attend monthly group practices, which is a different and more intense experience, because the sound continues when I take a breath. Each year I join an off-site retreat with a larger group. In order to safeguard concentration, there is no interpersonal communication whatsoever: just the sounding. This is very intense, and has a long-term impact on the psyche and on my concentration and awareness. For instance, for a period of time, I experience enhanced levels of sensitivity. Taste, smell, touch, vision, and most of all, the audio perception fare in altered, higher states of refinement and awareness. It's made me realize how little one needs to feel "full", if only sensitivity is awakened.

Another result I've experienced is the impressive physiological and mental resources that become available. I've learned to resist the temptation to take on more, add another part-time job for example, just because I can. That wouldn't serve the greater purpose, which is concentration and awareness.

Observing and moderating

It wasn't so long ago that, every day at around 10 a.m., I would head down from my desk to the cafeteria and grab a cappuccino. I'd hang out with my colleagues, have another cappuccino and order a third one to take away before returning to my desk. I would sit there and feel such a rush related to everything that needed to happen right now, if not yesterday, that I'd soon go down for another cappuccino just to manage the stress.

I am not sure what prompted me, but one day I sat down and went through that whole cycle in my head. What am I doing? Why? It didn't take me long to realize that my behavior did not require attention to be activated. I was on autopilot.

In fact, the reason I stood up at 10 a.m. was to stretch my legs and most of all to see my friends. I also found out that the stress I experienced wasn't due to some change that had occurred while I was at the cafeteria, but because the caffeine had changed me. I decided to test this assumption about cause and effect by ordering tea. It worked. So now I experience the benefits – social interaction – without the drawbacks.

Seeking out the good in the "bad"

I've realized that in order to introduce balance in life, it sometimes helps to look for activities that seem less pleasant, as these can help me to greater self-regulation. Work isn't always awesome. This is a fact. So, I deliberately seek to increase my capacity for dealing with those tasks that I either resent or don't feel 100 per cent equipped for, or that make me feel uncomfortable. Afterwards, I feel more resilient. Most of all, it lowers my barrier of aversion.

For example, for years, I have taken a three-minute cold shower every morning. The physical experience remains the same – initially, it's always initially unpleasant. But the mental one has evolved: I know the process, and that at the end of the three minutes, I'll be feeling good and not at all cold (rather the opposite). I see a parallel between this and those moments when I have to deal with a seemingly boring or otherwise unpleasant task. I know that after being in it for a minute, it will be fine.

Internal gender balance

Most of my young male managers today display behavior typically asso-ciated with what were previously considered a female style of leading – listening, teamwork, cooperation instead of competition, and so on. It brings a different level of interaction into the game, and more rest. People feel content and at ease, which is better for overall results and job satis-faction. Gender based role divisions haven't played a significant role in our team for a long time.

At home, I do the cleaning every Friday. We have two young children and by the end of the week the house is a total mess. I don't like it, and always feel resistance. So, I decided to treat the mess as an opportunity. I live in such an abstract world at work where it is rare to come about real grounding in the reality of life – nature, body, cycles. Sorting out the toys, folding the kids' clothes, cleaning up in the kitchen helps me con-nect with how things work in the material world. For me it's an important exercise and a rewarding one – and with pleasingly immediate results! Contentment to me is an effect of temperance.

Notes

1 www.redcrowmarketing.com/2015/09/10/many-ads-see-one-day/
2 Similarly, drinking alcohol can become an expression of a person's consum-ing attention to the spiritual dimension. But instead of consciously and delib-erately seeking contact directly with this dimension, drinking alcohol can become a substitute. C. G. Jung inspired Big Bill in Bill's construction of Alcohol Anonymous. Jung told him that the recovering alcoholic would need to recognize God, and indeed this is one of the 12 steps.
3 "Cyberbullying Statistics 2019" https://techjury.net/stats-about/cyberbullying/

4 www.gurlstalk.com/gurls/article/my-instagram-addiction/

5 The eyes representing the two Os; the line of the cheeks, eyebrows, and nose forming an M; D, E, and I shown in ears, nostrils, and mouth.

6 Alighieri, D. *The Divine Comedy II: Purgatory*, Canto XXIII: 10–12. Translation by the Rev. H.F. Cary, M.A. Urbana, IL: Project Gutenberg. Retrieved 5 June 2019 from www.gutenberg.org/ebooks/8795.

7 Furthermore, it points to the fact that it is not time only that makes us grow. If time is also filled by someone else's selfless wish to help, support, guide, stand by, suffer for, forgive, and encourage, then growth and development are quicker. Much of our growth depends on the attitude of intimate friends and partners. At the same time, a prayerful attitude to a beloved inner figure, as in the case of Nell, his wife, who prayed for the healing of her internalized inner man as much as for her dead husband, reaches out to the larger powers behind our development, and so heals her too. In that sense a couple is a unit.

8 New reference: Alighieri, D. *The Divine Comedy II: Purgatory*, Canto XXIV: 151–154. Translation by the Rev. H.F. Cary, M.A. Urbana, IL: Project Gutenberg. Retrieved 5 June 2019 from www.gutenberg.org/ebooks/8795.

9 The redemptive character of the suffering pertaining to temperance is emphasized and illustrated by Taylor and Finley in *Images of the Journey in Dante's Divine Comedy* (1997).

10 Alighieri, D. *The Divine Comedy II: Purgatory*, Canto XXIV: 149–150. Translation by the Rev. H.F. Cary, M.A. Urbana, IL: Project Gutenberg. Retrieved 5 June 2019 from www.gutenberg.org/ebooks/8795.

11 www.voedingscentrum.nl/encyclopedie/anorexia.aspx

12 Hougaard, R. and Carter, J. (2018). *The Mind of the Leader: How to Lead Yourself, Your People and Your Organization for Extraordinary Results*. Boston, MA: Harvard Business Review Press.

13 https://adaa.org/social-media-obsession

Chapter 9

Lust and chastity

In Dante's world lust is the last of the seven sins, the mildest and most forgivable. Lust and chastity are closest to Heaven because they are linked to love, the love in which one forgets oneself. Lust is about desire for immediate, indiscriminate sexual satisfaction. Chastity, on the other hand, fosters deliberate choice, suspense of satisfaction and commitment. Here lust is purged of its unconscious imperative. There is a difference between losing oneself to sex and losing the self to love. In the first there is a risk of disintegration, whereas the latter offers a chance of wholeness. Human love and relationship, love with lust and lust with love, are keys to transformation.

Both Church and State try to regulate lust. Many of the Calvinist reforms of sixteenth-century Geneva still exist in our modern civil and common law traditions. We are brought up to see sex as a potential enemy of productivity. So, we are taught to believe that if we have too much sex we cannot possibly become successful. On the other hand, leadership power, money and status are deemed as erotic. In Henry Kissinger's words: "Power is the ultimate aphrodisiac." So, what must be avoided at all costs in securing achievements, indulgence in sex and pleasure, is the promise of hard work. Translated to an organizational context, this argument means that if you work yourself up to an executive position, then your potency and power to attract potential sex will increase too. To say that men are prone to test this assumption is an open door, but do women with leadership power, in combination with good looks and sex appeal, experience more erotic satisfaction? Do they laugh more, flirt more and take longer lunch breaks? Do they find themselves asking the man, "How old *are* you?" Less powerful sisters suspect they do.

Although leaders I worked with may agree, they would add that lust *is* love. And love gives an appetite for life, not just for sex or for anything one-sided. Love is the fuel of ambition in a much broader sense and manifests in all areas of life. Chastity adds moderation and reason. Lust without chastity can bring about sudden, decisive actions, from personal infidelity to corporate strategy. The danger is that these decisions are not well thought through; they are not linked to reason, but are purely irrational, often erratic short-term decisions and actions. If not moderated, either by existing structures (which is what the Church tries to offer us), or by a discipline of chastity that says "let me sleep on this one", then irrational passion can turn into unreflected sense-making, motivating action with "because I feel like it". We see that sometimes in one-night stands as well as in the urge that motivates acquisitions of companies or corporate mergers. Lust motivates in a way that is different from greed. The major difference is that lust has no other reason to be than itself, it is its own object.

Lust and chastity in Dante's Purgatory

Dante and Virgil move upwards towards the last, seventh level of lust (*luxuria*) and chastity. The slopes become shorter and narrower as they encounter the fire that absorbs the lustful. They must walk one after the other. Virgil warns Dante that now they really must pay attention, because on their left they have the flames blasting from the inner wall and on their right the abyss. "Strict rein must in this place direct the eyes. A little swerving and the way is lost," he says.[1]

> So enter'd we upon our way,
> One before other; for, but singly, none
> That steep and narrow scale admits to climb.
>
> E'en as the young stork lifteth up his wing
> Through wish to fly, yet ventures not to quit
> The nest, and drops it – so in me.[2]

Virgil's warning to look out can be understood as topographical, which it no doubt is, but beyond that it also indicates the danger of lust. If you do not watch out, your eye will be caught in it and you will fall. It can happen in an instant, and may have disastrous effects. A third understanding is that Virgil means to say that you must walk the last bit alone. Each soul must climb up on its own and inside itself, no matter how much guidance and support it receives. A fourth understanding refers to the soul's loneliness in encountering sexual temptation. We will return to this point in the section dealing with psycho-spiritual aspects of lust and chastity. Finally, the looking out: to look and look well is preparation for the next stop, the Earthly Paradise, because looking plays a central role there. From then on Dante sees the world through Beatrice's eyes.

The lustful are purged by fire. They cleanse away their craving for sex, which they used to give into beyond reason and measure. A reminder of that neurotic obsession is reflected in their conduct and their prayer. The lustful run on the slope in opposite directions, one group to the left and the other to the right, and they kiss as they meet. They sing a hymn, "God of supreme clemency." At the conclusion of each hymn, they stop to cry out in loud voices, praising an example of chastity. For instance Mary, who exclaimed, "I know not a man." They then softly continue the hymn again. In this way, they relate different examples of chastity.

Fire is used sparingly by Dante. In Purgatory it is only at this final level that we meet the fire. Fire is the image of lust and at the same time its remedy, as it burns away lustful cravings. It is also an image of purity. The other side of fire (and lust) comes together in one single experience. This form of contact with the other, with Beatrice via Virgil, is precisely what finally persuades Dante to take the leap to go through the fire. Virgil coached Dante gently, telling him that although the fire burns, it will not kill him. And Virgil went through the fire first, offering to hold on to Dante's tunic, talking of Beatrice who is waiting on the other side, thereby keeping their connection alive for Dante when he was trembling and afraid. Eager to fly but afraid to leave is how Dante felt at this, the final level.

This is typical of the process of letting go of the rationality associated with the ego. But cleansing, or in this case burning away ego limitations, is a condition for attaining a full relationship with the soul. Beatrice is the soul figure of Dante. His longing for union, or integration in psychological terms, will win over fear, but not without the tormenting process of fire, about which Dante says: "I would have cast me into molten glass to cool me, when I enter'd; so intense rag'd the conflagrant mass."[3]

Love and lust – this is the very theme of the entire journey through Purgatory, and here these forces come together to unite Dante within himself. As the final, seventh "P" is erased by the Angel of Chastity, invisible to Dante because wrapped up in light so white it is blinding, Dante is free to enter the Earthly Paradise, where Beatrice awaits him and where the dualities no longer exist. Human reason is neither necessary nor sufficient for the right conduct. Love is greater. "Love, and do as you like" – because what you ought to do and what you want to do are now the same thing.[4] Before this transition takes place though, at the top of the steps, Virgil speaks:

Expect no more
Sanction of warning voice or sign from me,
Free of thy own arbitrement to choose,
Discreet, judicious. To distrust thy sense
Were henceforth error. I invest thee then
With crown and mitre, sovereign o'er thyself.[5]

Virgil, who as we know represents human reason and knowledge, has come to the end too. He can no longer offer Dante guidance because beyond the seventh level guidance follows inner feeling and knowing. Dante has arrived at the point where he has access to the source of guidance within himself – this is the transition. He now leads the way and Virgil follows him into the wood. This time it is not the dark wood in which Dante was lost at the onset of the journey, but Eden. Virgil leaves, and there is Beatrice. In what may be the most dramatic, moving passage of the entire *Comedy*, Beatrice says:

Observe me well. I am, in sooth, I am
Beatrice. What! and hast thou deign'd at last
Approach the mountain? knewest not, O man!
Thy happiness is whole?[6]

Personal developmental aspects of lust and chastity

In the public debate, lust and chastity in modern Western society are commonly linked to two different ways of relating to commitments, especially when engaging in intimate relationships. One stereotype is that women want fidelity (chastity) and men want liberty (lust). In my observation, this kind of duality and (sometimes interchangeable) division of inclinations can occur in all forms of relationships; it may even be a necessary aspect of intimate relationships and personal growth. It prevents security from ruining excitement and yet manages the bond between two people. This tension between union and separation is probably part and parcel of all living relationships and provides the energy that can become transformational for each individual.

Transformation in relationships such as marriage may occur when the bond between two people manages to hold the polarities together.[7] That bond is the love that goes beyond rationality – formal vows, for instance – and forms a kind of pact deep in the unconscious realms of the relationship. Murray Stein, a Jungian psychoanalyst in Zurich, states:

"Marriages that are transformative relationships have the effect of generating irrationally based images of wholeness and unity, which partners can relate to as essential and vitally important to life's meaning. These are not the images of an ideal couple, but images of integration that embody the opposites."[8]

Dante's journey reminds us that love is the key to transformation because love comprises the opposites. A person who cannot access that level of love may nevertheless long for it. This can lead to a driven pursuit of one thing or an experience that it is believed will bring it about. Addiction, a well-known phenomenon among psychoanalysts, is the quest for an object that is perfect and can undo feelings of despair. It betrays love, because it is obsessed as an external object that can never be fulfilled. It is a prison.[9] Love here means freedom from the limitation of one-sidedness. Sometimes we are all more afraid of freedom than of constraint.

Addiction to sex in the form of pornography can undo the tension between unity and separation that a relationship offers, and thus hinder development, psychologically and relationally. Unlike Dante's time, when pornography was available as drawings on secret leaflets, today pornography is characterized by readily available sex and does not require much effort to obtain – it is one click away. What is the effect of this influx of erotic imagery on couples' sex lives and relationships? Nothing could be more difficult to determine because although pornography may demystify "having sex", our most intimate feelings are still secret, sometimes even to the person who has them, despite the manifestation of how a feeling "looks". What can be established with some level of security, though, is that when pornography becomes addictive and is used compulsively, it tends to lead away from the real thing – excitement, arousal, desire and satisfaction in a relationship with a partner. Naomi Wolf, liberal feminist and author states:

> Does all this sexual imagery in the air mean that sex has been liberated – or is it the case that the relationship between the multi-billion-dollar porn industry, compulsiveness and sexual appetite has become like the relationship between agribusiness, processed foods, supersize portions and obesity? If your appetite is stimulated and fed by poor-quality material, it takes more junk to fill you up. People are not closer because of porn but further apart; people are not more turned on in their daily lives but less so.[10]

Psychologically speaking, addiction to pornography and autoerotic isolation are linked to a form of narcissism.[11] It is not the alpha narcissist that we encountered in pride, but counter-dependent narcissism. Characteristic of a counter-dependent narcissism, according to Jungian psychoanalysts Nancy Dougherty and Jacqueline West, is that it preserves a person and makes him or her "stay young" – the eternal youth. One frequently used image that illustrates major traits is that by Scottish playwright J. M. Barrie (1904) in *Peter Pan*: a motherless child who subsequently denies, often aggressively, the need of mothering, and instead develops a self-reliant but isolated can-do mentality and who flees into a world of lonely imagination.[12]

Jungian psychoanalyst Marie-Louise von Franz, in her interpretation of *The Little Prince* by Antoine de Saint Exupéry,[13] shows how *creativity* is part of the eternal youth image. She sees creativity as the other side of infantile pleasure and the world of imagination: the divine spark of creative genius. Without childish spontaneity, the ability to play and forget oneself, to let go and be yourself, there is no real creativity. Creativity is also an outcome of a balanced relationship between lust and chastity. Chastity can transform sexual energy from lethargy to creativity and move selfish love towards love in a relationship. This has important implications for development and leadership.

Leadership development through lust and chastity

There is no leadership without Eros. Eros, in Greek mythology, is the personification of love and psychologically represents the function of a relationship. As C. G. Jung says:

> Eros is a questionable fellow. . . . He belongs on one side to man's primordial animal nature which will endure as long as man has an animal body. On the other side he is related to the highest forms of the spirit. But he thrives only when spirit and instinct are in right harmony. If one or the other aspect is lacking to him, the result is injury or at least lopsidedness that may easily veer towards the pathological.[14]

People in leadership roles sometimes feel as if their whole being breathes this "questionable fellow". Eros leadership, in a context dominated by textbook rationale, enhances creativity between two parties. A decision made with a combination of lust and chastity, body and mind, instinct and spirit, is more cohesive. It supports creativity and progress, and offers ever new opportunities of finding unexpected solutions to old and new problems. The art of this form of feminine leadership is indeed its intrinsic, perpetual search for balance, again and again, in a circular way, reaching out for and working with greater and greater opposing powers, of which where each one is seeking to gain the upper hand. C. G. Jung defines these as follows:

> Where love reigns, there is no will to power; and where the will to power is paramount, love is lacking. The one is but the shadow of the other: the man who adopts the standpoint of Eros finds his compensatory opposite in the will to power, and that of the man who puts the accent on power is Eros.[15]

Love and power are mutually exclusive opposites when placed next to each other. This way of thinking has formed the basis for much decision-making by Western companies, for example, through outsized acquisitions. Power in the marketplace has been achieved largely at the expense of love in this same market. But love and power can come together in creativity, which is experienced and expressed in lust with chastity, in a vibrant, living relationship acknowledging and moving with the other.

Leaders working through presence and personality in this way may seem more vulnerable than those who take the safer route, using only rationality. Yet in times of change and upheaval of familiar structures, the safest place is in the now.[16] The present moment holds all the potential, it is the moment when the past and future come together. It is in the now that a person can make choices and express and manifest them in real time in relation to other people. The presence of mind required to optimally engage with the other in the now is supported by Eros through dialogue. Without Eros, no psychic energy is exchanged, instinctual connections are eliminated, and consequently the individual feels no emotional attachment. Lack of Eros may lead to over-emphasis on pure, precooked rationality, which potentially has a dehumanizing effect, and spills over in an attitude towards nature, animals and people that is careless and geared by a narrow wish for power.

Eros bears a similarity to numinosity,[17] the feeling of being in communion with the Other. These notions point to a central outcome of psychospiritual leadership development. It is such an important one because it works through all interconnected relationships and impacts both the individual leader and the entire surrounding network. Numinosity is a spiritual force that, when acknowledged, is the relationship between people, places and business.[18]

At this uppermost level of lust and chastity, we get a glimpse of Dante's ultimate experience of Heaven at the very end of his journey through Purgatory. This is the experience of unity and knowing that the whole of the universe comes together in one experience, when the powers of intellect and instinct are equally balanced:

A l'alta fantasia qui mancò possa;
ma già volgeva il mio disio e 'l *velle*,
sì come rota ch'igualmente è mossa,
l'amor che move il sole e l'altre stelle.[19]

Reflections on chastity

Aukje Nauta

Why I listen and observe

In high school, I was very shy and self-conscious. I would anxiously observe classmates: who was talking to whom, who was being excluded, who was some kind of leader, which couples were dating, and so on. Most of all, I spent vast amounts of energy listening, and assessing my own place in the group.

This is quite a normal developmental stage in puberty, especially among teenage girls. But for me that experience was formative. It determined my choice of study and later my professional life. It's why I studied organizational psychology: to better understand interpersonal dynamics, why people behave as they do and how this impacts the workplace.

Since completing my studies in Groningen, I have published on HR related topics including conflict, negotiation and mediation in organizations, social comparison, teamwork and sustainable employability. I'm currently engaged as a part-time professor at Leiden University, with a special assignment, "Enhancing individuals in a dynamic work context". My focus is creating a bridge between the worlds of science and work, in companies and organizations.

Factor Five Consultancy

In 2010, I started a consultancy firm called Factor Five Consultancy. The name is derived from the fifth of the Big Five personality traits: "openness to experience", or sometimes also called "intellectual autonomy". People who score high on this trait are curious and very open to change. Our work is geared towards renewing working relationships positively, with respect for diversity and inclusion. We work mainly with two tools: dialogue and customized roles, tailored to the employee which we call an "I-deal". It's formed by employer and employee working together to determine the right fit for the employee and is an essential tool for creating a foundation of strong working relationships.

This kind of personal approach to defining professional profiles is increasingly important. This is in part due to the tension that exists between the system which regulates educational institutions and the demands of the labor market. Take secondary vocational educations, which are regulated by strict curricular criteria. Developing new criteria takes seven years! But the companies seeking to hire the graduates are constantly looking for different things: their criteria change every year. This makes it essential that each individual's personal profile is considered when they are employed in a particular role, and that there is room to learn from practice on a daily basis.

An unusual off-site

I tend to work with both private and public organizations. For example, I guided team-building sessions of several management teams. We recently had an off-site with one of these teams. Normally these are conducted over two days, but this time it was one, long, intense day. We had agreed that this off-site would focus on the team members' personal situations before working on strategic issues. The team was responsible for stimulating and improving internal and external cooperation, and they wanted to approach the issue in a loving way. They felt that they needed to develop their empathy for each other first in order to facilitate this.

The team consists of a group of six individuals between 45 and 60 years of age, three women and three men. We started out by having them share what was going on in their private lives and what emotions they were experiencing as a result. These were open and very personal exchanges and the atmosphere was intimate. Finally, the last person told his story, but his words were superficial and he did not open up. Given that he is the most senior member of the team and their direct superior, this was quite uncomfortable for the others. I had to intervene. I instinctively felt it to be my job not to let him get away with it – for everyone's sake. So, I stated his name and asked, "But how do you *feel* right now?"

He started crying. He then told us about his sister, whose young son had committed suicide. I too started crying, because I was overwhelmed by emotion at this tragedy. The rest of the group was extremely supportive, and remained respectfully quiet. Once the emotions had settled,

I suggested a break in order for his colleagues to share their personal experiences and sincere empathy.

Next was a presentation by a new team leader in charge of hundreds of people. She told a very personal story about her experiences in the role and the challenges she faced trying to lead her large team. This intermezzo worked well as it gave us all a moment to concentrate on something more external and objective, a counterpoint to the deep opening and emotion we had shared. Later, we went on to discuss the importance of crafting roles based on talent, and talked about introducing new ways of working based on task-oriented activities.

This work truly requires dialogue. By dialogue, I mean a conversation around what really matters in the situation. This kind of conversation takes courage, and requires participants to be ready to face confrontation while remaining vulnerable, as well as allowing space to voice doubt and insecurity.

Anxiety, emotion and love

Such dialogues both awaken and resolve anxiety. Personally, I've learned that self-doubt is part of my life and that I have anxieties, uncertainties and fears that won't go away by denying them. Instead, I try my best to acknowledge this reality and better understand their underlying meaning or message. High-quality dialogues and a sense of humor help achieve that.

As for love in my personal life, it does not manifest in a traditional form, because my lover is also committed to another woman. It is not always easy – what is? – yet, we have made a deliberate choice to build on our relationship and develop within it. Clear appointments and suspense serve to further our relationship. For me it is a learning process that has implications far beyond the bedroom.

Incorporating personal emotions creates space for greater compassion in the workplace. It requires that we really see the other, every other person, not just when it's easy or convenient. Only then do we take care of other people's interests, as well as our own.

Attending to your own interests as well as those of others are not mutually exclusive concepts. That is precisely why I promote the formation of 'I-deals' between employers or clients, and their employees. The I-deal is the smallest building block; it creates a working relationship in which both parties show their pro-social, loving side. This forms a foundation. If we choose to give and take with love in the workplace, both employees and organization flourish.

Notes

1 Alighieri, D. *The Divine Comedy II: Purgatory*, Canto XXV: 119–120. Translation by the Rev. H.F. Cary, M.A. Urbana, IL: Project Gutenberg. Retrieved 5 June 2019 from www.gutenberg.org/ebooks/8795.
2 Alighieri, D. *The Divine Comedy II: Purgatory*, Canto XXV: 7–12. Translation by the Rev. H.F. Cary, M.A. Urbana, IL: Project Gutenberg. Retrieved 5 June 2019 from www.gutenberg.org/ebooks/8795.
3 Alighieri, D. *The Divine Comedy II: Purgatory*, Canto XXVII: 49–51. Translation by the Rev. H.F. Cary, M.A. Urbana, IL: Project Gutenberg. Retrieved 5 June 2019 from www.gutenberg.org/ebooks/8795.
4 Alighieri, D. *The Divine Comedy II: Purgatory*, p. 288. Quoting Saint Augustine.
5 Alighieri, D. *The Divine Comedy II: Purgatory*, Canto XXVII: 138–143. Translation by the Rev. H.F. Cary, M.A. Urbana, IL: Project Gutenberg. Retrieved 5 June 2019 from www.gutenberg.org/ebooks/8795.
6 Alighieri, D. *The Divine Comedy II: Purgatory*, Canto XXX: 73–76. Translation by the Rev. H.F. Cary, M.A. Urbana, IL: Project Gutenberg. Retrieved 5 June 2019 from www.gutenberg.org/ebooks/8795.
7 See e.g., Perel (2007, 2017).
8 Stein (1998), p. 101.
9 About that prison, Tyminski writes: "A seeker who cannot help himself, cannot stop himself, and will give anything in his quest for thrill-seeking immortality. Near-total unconsciousness afflicts conditions of addiction and compulsion, resulting in a loss of ego as a person mindlessly pursues 'substance' that is golden, powerful, and irresistible. The illusion of such a perfect object seduces the addict into darkness, where he or she hopes to forget some awful pain. Defensive omnipotence and splitting help to maintain the false belief that the perfect object can be concretely – physically – held and turned into a form of a manic reparation for feelings of hopelessness and limitation" (2009, p. 58).
10 Naomi Wolf, in *The Beauty Myth*, states that pornography does not liberate women sexually, but rather confines them to a compelling ideal of beauty. She makes an interesting link between the ideal of beauty and female empowerment: "The more legal and material hindrances women have broken through, the more strictly and heavily and cruelly images of female beauty have come to weigh upon us. . . . During the past decade, women breached the power structure; meanwhile, eating disorder rose exponentially and cosmetic surgery became the fastest-growing specialty. . . . Pornography became the main media category, ahead of legitimate films and records combined, and thirty-three thousand American women told researchers that they would rather lose ten to fifteen pounds than achieve any other goal. . . . More women have more money and power and scope and legal recognition than we have ever had before; but in terms of how we feel about ourselves physically, we may actually be worse off than our unliberated grandmothers" (2002, p. 10).
11 See, for example, Kernberg, O. (1998). *Love Relations: Normality and Pathology*. New Haven, CT: Yale University Press.
12 A *puella* woman, an eternal girl, shares these characteristic with the *puer* (young boy), but may seem more passive in that she tends to absorb more from her environment than the *puer*, for instance, projections, hence

inordinately adapting her looks and behavior in order to please. She tends to avoid getting engaged in personal relationships. Whomever she meets, there will always be a hair in the soup, something that makes her reject her partner and believe that instead there is another flawless person waiting around the next corner. She may be attractive, imaginative, sparkling and full of energy, but yet meeting others without ever making enduring contact, let alone creating real intimacy and in-depth sharing in an emotional way. She simply cannot, however much she longs for it. Linda Schierse Leonard, in *On The Way to the Wedding: Transforming The Love Relationship*, identifies four modes of the eternal girl: (a) adaptation to projections to please the partner; (b) retreat from life into inner fantasy; (c) continuous moves from one possibility to another; (d) self-destructive rebellion against convention (Boulder, CO: Shambhala Publications, 1986, p. 253).

13 Von Franz, M.-L. (1998). *The Problem of the Puer Aeternus*. Toronto: Inner City Books.
14 Jung, C. G. (1977). *Collected Works 7*, paragraph 32.
15 CW7: *Two Essays on Analytical Psychology*.
16 Edmondson, A. (2018). *The Fearless Organization: Creating Psychological Safety in the Workplace for Learning, Innovation and Growth*. New York: Wiley.
17 Such experience has been identified and studied in different areas of the psychology of religion. Rudolf Otto, a twentieth-century German theologian, describes the double-sidedness of a numinous experience as *mysterium tremendum et mysterium fascinans*, fearful and fascinating mystery. In *The Idea of the Holy* (1958) Otto defines as a numinous experience a non-rational feeling whose object is outside of oneself, so the person feels in communion with something wholly other.
18 In *Dream of Love* (2018) I experimented with the narrative form of a novel in pursuit of capturing that particular feel of the energy (that is both wave and particle) which informs consciousness of unity in creation.
19 This excerpt is in the original language used by Dante to write *The Divine Comedy*: Italian. Helpful translations to English include those by John Ciardi (2003), Dorothy L. Sayers (1955) and Allen Mandelbaum (1984).

Chapter 10

The rise of feminine leadership

Feminine leadership is not a fixed thing. It is neither a commodity nor a position. In this book, it is understood to mean what leaders do when they take charge of themselves in a given situation, make choices about how to act, and take decisions about the direction and purpose of these actions. In most cases it has implications for other people. In that sense, leaders are responsible for others as well. Feminine leadership is an aspect of all forms of leadership because it acknowledges and consciously attends to the different dimensions of the leadership process. In what follows I will reflect on the nature of these dimensions.

Psycho-spiritual aspects of the false self and the true self

Who could possibly object to the notion that the world today would benefit massively from leaders who took the undertakings of feminine leadership seriously and invested in exploring the core of the matter rather than making obvious surface values the whole point? I think most leaders would agree with this – and remember – everyone is a leader. It's just that it is challenging and oftentimes the priority seems to be anything except "exploring the core of the matter". This is where psychological work comes into the picture.

The false self establishes conventions and the institutions that uphold these conventions. It fits in. But, as long as the false self remains uncharted, it operates unconsciously and automatically: it guides you. Psychologically this is recognized in complexes, habits of mind and dependencies. These in turn often stem from your conventional image of how you "should" be as a leader, the persona. It tells you what to do and what not to do, what is possible and not, what is right and wrong. The false self further puts you at risk of identifying with the collective stereotypes of "leader". You risk being trapped and defined by it because it is reinforced by formal education and corporate culture, and it colludes with the persona. This double command by the false self makes it very persuasive and difficult to break out of. The false self strives to dominate and so demonstrates a kind of compulsion *not to* surrender. If you do not pay attention to and become aware of your false self, it will tie you to a limited perspective about yourself and the world around you. This significantly compromises your capacity to lead successfully. At least in the view of the word.

However, in the long run, attachment to the false self cannot do away with a felt undercurrent of dissatisfaction and limitation. This is a subtle reminder of the true self, however, which tries to call attention its way. The true self brings to life the longing for peace and serenity. It offers glimpses of timeless freedom. It speaks with the voice of your soul. It speaks of love, harmony and beauty. In all of creation. Blissful clarity. It can be tempting to try to skip over the false self and simply give undivided attention to that beautiful feeling. But it is a mistake not to examine the false self, because what is unknown cannot be renounced.[1]

What is the chief Sufi method for annihilation, *Fana?* In the practice offered by Sufi mystic and Pir-o-Murshid Hazrat Inayat Khan, the two most fundamental factors are the breath and the willing surrender, or renunciation. But at the core of this is the treasure of concentration, resulting from the training of the mind/heart. Hazrat Inayat Khan:

> In concentration lies the secret of all things. What is meant by concentration is the change of identification of the soul, so that it may lose the false conception of identification and identify itself with the true self instead of the false self. This is what is meant by self-realization. Once a person realizes his self by the proper way of concentration, of contemplation, of meditation, he has understood the essence of all religions. Because all religions are only different ways that lead to one truth, and that truth is self-realization.[2]

The true self, or soul, comprehends the bigger picture instantly, because it is united with it.

The true self is founded in unity, and therefore it views the world from an inclusive perspective. It perpetually adds insights. As a result, it has the capacity to help you break out of your false self and that of the collective consciousness.

So it is very understandable that all mystical teachings emphasize the value of a personal journey of self-exploration. The Sufi mysticism, which is part of my personal spirituality, describes different aspects of the false self, called the *Nafs*. The envious, greedy, gluttonous and, God forbid, the lustful. There are several parallels between Sufism and Dante's journey.[3]

Dante's guidance for feminine leadership

Dante's imaginative journey through Purgatory is a psychological and a spiritual way projected on to the alluring image of Beatrice. As we have seen, the sins and virtues are not only the tasks on a Christian checklist. They are a system for thinking about who you are, what triggers you, and how you can use this knowledge to develop as a person. Dante's example teaches us not only that it is possible to overcome these hang-ups and limitations, but also *how to look* at the challenges in order to tackle them successfully. He shows us how to live with duality without getting caught in mutually excluding polarities.

Dante stands in life with a strong sense of the present, but he maintains a long-term perspective. His life journey is characterized by curiosity, courage, astonishment, passion and trust in the process. His descriptions of personalities in Purgatory show an attitude of detached involvement. We recognize this as detachment from the immediate demands of the false self, and the continual involvement of the true self. There are moments in our lives when these positions come together, and Dante reminds us of that. Freedom is to be fully involved in the process of what is happening in the present, and yet at the same time to be detached from any desired outcome.

Freedom comes from consciously and responsibly managing the tension between extremes, the opposing ends in a continuum. The connection between Dante and feminine leadership is that they operate on an axis of the same two sets of paired opposites. The first set is horizontal and consists of the relationship between intrinsic thinking and feeling on the one hand and the extrinsic demands and expectations that confront you on the other. It is reflected in the way you balance your psychological make-up, including complexes, dependencies and habits of mind, with external demands such as deadlines and difficult colleagues.

The second paired set is vertical. It consists of the relationship between the false self and the true self. This axis is more subtle and spiritual. It is critical for all forms of leadership to know how the energy of this vortex works in alignment. To balance these is a strictly personal endeavor: you must discover it for yourself. Too much of the true self leads to too much detachment from the immediate, too little urgency and concrete direction. Too much of the false self leads to short-term, manipulative, selfish and unethical actions.

In addition, this form of balancing requires a practiced sense of timing and connection with the horizontal dimension. The double balancing of the horizontal and the vertical dimensions is necessary for gradual integration in all areas of life.

Like Dante, modern leaders invest their time and energy in reflecting on themselves. Just as Dante did, successful leaders accept intuition, the non-rational perceiver in our psyche, as a major source of information. Accepting that there are no simple solutions, they tend to see personal development and growth as a circular, continuous process that needs attention on both vertical and horizontal planes.

The professional implication of feminine leadership is that you create meaning by acting from your biography. It is characterized by striving to integrate personal, emotional, aesthetic, ethical, existential and spiritual dimensions of being and behaving in the leadership function. By knowing your self (horizontally) and what the spiritual and the ethical principles that guide your decision-making (vertically), you become able to reflect on and assess the situation as it is and to take action accordingly.

Feminine leadership endorses the unique and the general, the local and the global, the personal and that which is shared by all humanity. Its ethical guideline is "openness", and this permeates its process, which is dialogical, reflective, and transparent.

It is when we interface with other people and colleagues that responsibility is enacted. Leaders who work through the horizontal dimension bring more consciousness to daily personal contacts. They create a way of being together that forms the basis for more widespread interactions leading to innovation, continuous transformation and development – inherently holding the capacity for trust in life. This is key – trust in the process even though you do not know the outcome. In practice, this means that it fosters transparent communication and curiosity along with entrepreneurship. These are essential requirements in a transcultural, global marketplace that demands flexibility and adaptability.

At the beginning of this book I pointed out that to give archetypal expression to experience is a way to interact consciously with the collective. Archetypal images are shared by all cultures, and while they are not people, their qualities can be emulated and thereby activated in the collective. It facilitates our participation in creation. Using imagery connects the larger picture of the outer, shared realm with our innermost being, and enables us to resolve this relationship within our own capacity. It is a way to translate your personal experiences into a much broader perspective and understand yourself as part of a larger picture, because *you are* part of a greater whole. Leadership is, after all, not a solo mission, but a role inextricably interwoven with the other. Moreover, modern leadership is ungendered, and all-gendered. All leaders have feminine qualities and harnessing these is imperative for meaningful, courageous leadership. Understanding this consciously, and interacting with it, inevitably creates harmony, and builds better relationships. It enables you as a leader to intrinsically act on a larger scale, in contrast to only focusing on a limited personal outlook.

In this way, leaders play a critical role in the transformation of the business community and society. They all contribute to that shift of consciousness that is inevitably approaching. The individuation process undertaken by the individual also plays a role in that process at large, perhaps a microscopic one, but still, without it no change will occur. Or to put it differently, organizations change because of the individuals who form them and the development they go through.

Companies and organizations are a very important part of our society. It is unsurprising that business leaders are often looked to for guidance and help in existential questions such as global warming and global recession in financial crises. We hope and expect that such leaders will be able to turn the tide and create new opportunities – business opportunities, but also breakthroughs in areas that relate to the safety of civic society. We want leaders to work courageously to foster good governance, and create a unilateral model that embraces more diversity and is more open than any model in the past. We need leaders who understand how we all depend upon one another and act to create a more balanced and virtuous ways of living. Leaders who have achieved governance over themselves, who are striving for self-realization and who know, experience and act from the power of the intrinsically feminine, can offer such leadership.

Notes

1 Jironet, K. (2002). *The Image of Spiritual Liberty in the Western Sufi Movement Following Hazrat Inayat Khan*. Leuven: Peeters.
2 Hazrat Inayat Khan (1988). *The Sufi Message. Volume VI: The Alchemy of Happiness*. New Delhi: Motilal Banasidass. p. 167.
3 See for example Corbin, H. (1998). *Alone with the Alone*. Princeton, NJ: Princeton University Press.

References

Alighieri, D. (1949). *The Divine Comedy I: Hell*. Translation by Dorothy L. Sayers. London: Penguin Classics.

Alighieri, D. (1955). *The Divine Comedy II: Purgatory*. Translation by Dorothy L. Sayers. London: Penguin Classics.

Alighieri, D. (1962). *The Divine Comedy III: Paradise*. Translation by Dorothy L. Sayers. London: Penguin Classics.

Alighieri, D. (1969). *La Vita Nuova*. Translation by Barbara Reynolds. London: Penguin Classics.

Alighieri, D. (2003). *The Divine Comedy: The Inferno, The Purgatorio and the Paradiso*. Translation by John Ciardi. New York: New American Library.

Barrie, J. M. (1999). Peter Hollindale (Introduction and Notes). ed. *Peter Pan in Kensington Gardens and Peter and Wendy*. Cambridge: Oxford University Press. Based on J. M. Barrie's play *Peter Pan; or, The Boy Who Wouldn't Grow Up* (1904).

Beard, M. (2018). *Women and Power: A Manifesto*. London: Profile Books.

Cooper Ramo, J. (2016). *The Seventh Sense: Power, Fortune, and Survival in the Age of Networks*. New York: Little, Brown & Company.

Corbin, H. (1998). *Alone with the Alone*. Princeton, NJ: Princeton University Press.

Davies, W. (2019). *Nervous States: Democracy and the Decline of Reason*. New York: W.W. Norton & Company.

Dehue, T. (2009). *De Depressie-Epidemie*. Groningen: Uitgeverij Augustus.

Dickens, C. (1994). *David Copperfield*. London: Penguin.

Dougherty, N. and West, J. (2007). *The Matrix and Meaning of Character: An Archetypal and Developmental Approach*. London: Routledge.

Edmondson, A. (2018). *The Fearless Organization: Creating Psychological Safety in the Workplace for Learning, Innovation and Growth*. New York: Wiley.

Fromm, E. (1994). *Escape From Freedom*. New York: Holt Paperbacks.

Fukuyama, F. (2018). *Identity: The Demand for Dignity and the Politics of Resentment*. New York: Farrar, Straus and Giroux.

Gates, M. (2019). *The Moment of Lift: How Empowering Women Changes the World*. New York: Flatiron Books.

Girard, R. (2004). *Oedipus Unbound: Selected Writings on Rivalry and Desire*. Edited by Mark R. Anspach. Stanford: Stanford University Press.

Greenspan, A. (2002). *Federal Reserve Board's Semiannual Monetary Policy Report to The Congress*, 16 July. Washington, DC: Federal Reserve Board.

Guggenbühl-Craig, A. (1971). *Power in the Helping Professions*. Putnam, CT: Spring Publications.

Hogenson, G. B. (2009). Synchronicity and moments of meeting. *Journal of Analytical Psychology*, 54(2): 183–197.

Holiday, R. (2014). *The Obstacle Is the Way: The Timeless Art of Turning Trials into Triumph*. New York: Portfolio.

Hood, R. Jr., Hill, P. and Spilka, B. (2009). *The Psychology of Religion: An Empirical Approach*. New York: Guilford Press.

Hougaard, R. and Carter, J. (2018). *The Mind of the Leader: How to Lead Yourself, Your People and Your Organization for Extraordinary Results*. Boston, MA: Harvard Business Review Press.

Jacobi, J. (1959). *Complex, Archetype, Symbol in the Psychology of C.G. Jung*. London: Routledge & Kegan Paul.

Jacobi, M. (1984). *The Analytical Encounter: Transference and Human Relationship*. Toronto: Inner City Books.

James, W. (1890). *The Principles of Psychology*. Boston, MA: Henry Holt.

Jironet, K. (2002). *The Image of Spiritual Liberty in the Western Sufi Movement Following Hazrat Inayat Khan*. Leuven: Peeters.

Jironet, K. (2009). *Sufi Mysticism into the West: Life and Leadership of Hazrat Inayat Khan's Brothers 1927–1967*. Leuven: Peeters.

Jironet, K. (2018). *Dream of Love*. Sheridan, WY: Genoa House.

Jung, C. G. (1966a). *Symbols of Transformation: Collected Works 5*. Princeton, NJ: Bollingen.

Jung, C. G. (1966b). *Two Essays in Analytical Psychology: Collected Works 7*. Princeton, NJ: Bollingen.

Jung, C. G. (1966c). *The Structure and Dynamics of the Psyche: Collected Works 8*. Princeton, NJ: Bollingen.

Kaplan, R. and Kaiser, R. B. (2009). Stop overdoing your strengths. *Harvard Business Review*, 87(2): 100–103.

Kernberg, O. (1998). *Love Relations: Normality and Pathology*. New Haven, CT: Yale University Press.

Khan, H. I. (1988). *The Sufi Message Volume VI: The Alchemy of Happiness*. New Delhi: Motilal Banarsidass.

Klein, M. (1988). *Envy and Gratitude and Other Works 1946–1963*. Reading: Cox and Wyman.

Kromme, C. (2017). *Humanification: Go Digital, Stay Human*. Gloucester: The Choir Press.

Laloux, F. (2014). *Reinventing Organizations: A Guide to Creating Organizations Inspired by the Next Stage in Human Consciousness*. Brussels: Nelson Parker.

Lückerath-Rovers, M. (2009). *The Dutch Female Board Index 2008*. Rotterdam: Erasmus Institute Monitoring and Compliance.

Luke, H. (1989). *Dark Wood to White Rose: Journey and Transformation in Dante's Divine Comedy*. New York: Parabola.

Mandelbaum, A. (1984). *The Divine Comedy of Dante Alighieri: Purgatorio*. New York: Bantam

Millon, T. and Davis, R. D. (1996). *Disorders of Personality: DSM-IV and Beyond*. New York: Wiley.

Obama, M. (2018). *Becoming*. New York: Crown Publishing Group.

Otto, R. (1958). *The Idea of The Holy: An Inquiry into the Non Rational Factor in the Idea of the Divine and its Relation to the Rational*. Oxford: Oxford University Press.

Ovid (1922). *Metamorphoses*, Book 3. Translation by Brookes More. Boston, MA: Cornhill.

Perel, E. (2007). *Mating in Captivity*. New York: HarperCollins.

Perel, E. (2017). *The State of Affairs: Rethinking Infidelity*. New York: Harper.

Samuels, A. (2006). Transference/countertransference. In R. Papadopoulos (ed.) *The Handbook of Jungian Psychology*. London: Routledge.

Samuels, A., Shorter, B. and Plaut, F. (1986). *A Critical Dictionary of Jungian Analysis*. London: Routledge.

Schierse Leonard, L. (2001). *On The Way to the Wedding: Transforming The Love Relationship*. Boston, MA: Shambala.

Sedgwick, D. (2005). *The Wounded Healer: Countertransference from a Jungian Perspective*. London: Routledge.

Seemiller, C. and Grace, M. (2018). *Generation Z: A Century in the Making*. London: Routledge.

Stein, M. (1996). *Practicing Wholeness*. New York: Continuum.

Stein, M. (1998). *Transformation: Emergence of the Self*. College Station, TX: A&M University Press.

Stein, M. (2003). *In MidLife*. Putnam, CT: Spring Publications.

Steinbeck, J. (1994). *The Pearl*. London: Penguin Classics.

Taylor, C. and Finley, P. (1997). *Images of the Journey in Dante's Divine Comedy*. New Haven, CT: Yale University Press.

Tyminski, R. (2009). Fleeced: A perspective from antiquity on contemporary addictions. *Jung Journal: Culture and Psyche*, 3(3): 52–68.

Ulanov, A. and Ulanov, B. (2008). *Cinderella and Her Sisters: The Envied and the Envying*. Einsiedeln: Daimon Verlag.

von Franz, M.-L. (1998). *The Problem of the Puer Aeternus*. Toronto: Inner City Books.

Winnicott, D. W. (1975). *Through Paediatrics to Psychoanalysis, Collected Papers*. London: Karnac Books.

Wolf, N. (2002). *The Beauty Myth: How Images of Beauty Are Used Against Women*. New York: HarperCollins.

Index